Business and Industry

EDITORS

William R. Childs
Scott B. Martin
Wanda Stitt-Gohdes

VOLUME 3

CORPORATE GOVERNANCE
to ENTREPRENEURSHIP

MARSHALL CAVENDISH
NEW YORK · TORONTO · LONDON · SYDNEY

Marshall Cavendish
99 White Plains Road
Tarrytown, New York 10591-9001

www.marshallcavendish.com

© 2004 Marshall Cavendish Corporation

Library of Congress Cataloging-in-Publication Data

Business and industry / editors, William R. Childs, Scott B. Martin, Wanda Stitt-Gohdes.
     p. cm.
   Includes bibliographical reference and index.
   Contents: v. 1. Accounting and Bookkeeping to Burnett, Leo--v. 2. Business Cycles to Copyright--
v. 3. Corporate Governance to Entrepreneurship--v. 4. Environmentalism to Graham,
Katharine--v. 5. Great Depression to Internship--v. 6. Inventory to Merrill Lynch--
v. 7. Microeconomics to Philip Morris Companies--v. 8. Price Controls to Sarnoff, David--
v. 9. Savings and Investment Options to Telecommuting--v. 10. Temporary Workers to Yamaha--
v. 11. Index volume
   ISBN 0-7614-7430-7 (set)--ISBN 0-7614-7433-1 (v. 3)
    1. Business--Encyclopedias. 2. Industries--Encyclopedias. I. Childs, William R., 1951-II. Martin,
Scott B., 1961-III. Stitt-Gohdes, Wanda.

HF1001 .B796 2003
338'.003--dc21   2002035156

Printed in Italy

06 05 04 03 5 4 3 2 1

MARSHALL CAVENDISH
Editorial Director   Paul Bernabeo
Production Manager   Alan Tsai

Produced by The Moschovitis Group, Inc.

THE MOSCHOVITIS GROUP
President, Publishing Division Valerie Tomaselli
Executive Editor   Hilary W. Poole
Associate Editor   Sonja Matanovic
Design and Layout   Annemarie Redmond
Illustrator   Richard Garratt
Assistant Illustrator   Zahiyya Abdul-Karim
Photo Research   Gillian Speeth
Production Associates   K. Nura Abdul-Karim, Rashida Allen
Editorial Assistants   Christina Campbell, Nicole Cohen, Jessica Rosin
Copyediting   Carole Campbell
Proofreading   Paul Scaramazza
Indexing   AEIOU, Inc.

Alphabetical Table of Contents

PHOTO CREDITS

Corporate Governance

Corporate governance is the delicate process of aligning the interests of owners and management. A great deal is at stake, including jobs, investor confidence, and spectacular sums of money. The corruption and scandals of the first years of the twenty-first century illustrated how this process has failed at the cost of investor mistrust, bankruptcies, and the criminal indictment of managers who gave in to temptation.

A corporation is a stockholder-owned business that has rights and responsibilities as if it were a person. These include the ability to sign contracts, legal protections, and the requirement to pay taxes. A corporation may also be sued or face criminal charges for wrongdoing. Corporations maximize the profits of shareholders by hiring specialists to make business decisions; the healthy operation of a corporation requires a balance between trust and accountability.

Stockholders, Boards, and Managers

The corporate governance structure involves three different groups: stockholders, the board of directors, and management. Anyone can become an owner of a publicly traded corporation by purchasing one or more shares of stock. These shares grant the owner a portion of any profits generated by the company and, in most cases, voting rights to retain or fire management.

Owning stock in large public corporations presents several problems. First, most people own stock through mutual funds that pool money from many investors to hire expert management at low costs. This has the benefit of maximizing long-term results through diversification (the purchase of stocks of many companies). The downside of this strategy is that mutual funds often own

See also:
Accounting and Bookkeeping; Business Ethics; Corporate Social Responsibility; Corporation.

In May 2002 billionaire Warren Buffett makes an appearance at a Dairy Queen diner in Omaha, Nebraska, to chat with shareholders of his company, Berkshire Hathaway. Omaha was host for Berkshire Hathaway's annual shareholders meeting, described by Buffett as "Woodstock for Capitalists."

Board of Directors' Practices

	Good governance	*Poor governance*
Origin of the board	Majority of board from outside corporation	Minority of board from outside corporation
Board's ties to management	Independent; no ties to management	Financial ties to management
Stock ownership by the board	Board members are significant shareholders	Board members hold little or no stock in corporation
Compensation of the board	Significant portion of compensation is stock-related	Compensated only with cash
Formal evaluations of the board	Yes	No
Board response to investor requests for information on governance issues	Responsive	Unresponsive

tens of billions of dollars worth of stocks and regularly buy and sell them; thus many investors are not aware of what stock they own. Also, few investors have a detailed knowledge of the industries they are invested in. This hampers their ability to objectively evaluate the performance of the managers hired to run each company. The fact that investors must rely on the honesty of corporate accounting statements makes this task even more challenging.

Boards of directors were developed to alleviate these problems and ensure that management acts in the best interest of the owners. Boards have several functions, including evaluating management, overseeing the business decisions of the company, and providing advice and counsel to management.

The average board of directors in the United States has 15 members, typically with business backgrounds. Members spend about two weeks throughout the year meeting with management. Sitting on a board of directors is attractive because the pay ranges from $10,000 to $50,000 per year for a small commitment of time.

Management's function is to make the business decisions for the owners. Stockholders rely on the board of directors to select specialists who will maximize profits and run the corporation responsibly. The leading manager is often referred to as the chief executive officer, or CEO. The CEO is selected by the board and approved by a vote of the stockholders. Most corporations also hold an annual vote where members of management must win majority approval to continue in their positions.

Economists and businesspeople have always been concerned about the relationship between ownership and management. Stockholders are risking their money and must trust management to operate with integrity. The fundamental problem is separation of ownership from control, which exists when no single shareholder or group of shareholders owns enough shares of stock to control management. Without this separation, managers may pursue their own objectives, including personal wealth or fame, rather than serve the stockholders.

Theory versus Practice

In theory, the relationship between management and ownership should work well for several reasons. First, competition in the marketplace should bankrupt inefficient companies. Second, corporations often link management pay to the profits of the company. Third, institutional investors, including mutual funds and pension systems, often purchase large blocks of shares and have both the expertise and a strong incentive to monitor management. Nevertheless, experts assert that corporate governance has grown dysfunctional. This situation is illustrated by contrasting the functions of the boards with the way they actually operate.

The primary purpose of a board of directors is to oversee management. However, most American boards are chaired, or led, by the CEO of the company. This creates a conflict of interest by placing the CEO in charge of evaluating his own performance.

The process of selecting board members often exacerbates this situation. In theory, selection is done democratically through the creation of a nominating committee to make selections when needed. The full board then votes on these recommendations, with a subsequent vote by stockholders. In practice, the majority of board openings are filled by the recommendation of the chair of the board. As the chair is also the CEO in most corporations, management is selecting the members of the boards, not the owners.

Corporate boards are also lax in protecting the interests of the owners because board members receive their compensation in spite of the performance of the company; thus they have little direct incentive to provide strict supervision. In addition, many directors serve on multiple boards and have full-time jobs of their own. Thus, they may lack the inclination or the time to aggressively defend the interests of owners.

The role of information further weakens the position of board members. Their position requires them to have accurate and timely data about company operations. This information is provided by management, making the board dependent on the very people it is supposed to monitor and giving management a means to downplay or conceal potential or actual problems. Taken together, these conditions make corporate governance problematic at best.

The Compensation Issue

One of the functions of the board of directors is to evaluate and recommend the compensation for management. Since many members of the board are picked by the CEO, conflict of interest arises.

Critics point to a variety of evidence that executive pay is out of line with performance. For example, a *New York Times* poll about CEO pay in relation to corporate profits and stock performance in 2001 showed that pay increased during a year of poor performance: overall profits dropped 35 percent

and stock value dropped 13 percent, but CEO pay increased by 7 percent. A *BusinessWeek* survey provided further information that executive compensation has escalated dramatically. In 1980 the average CEO earned roughly 42 times more that the average worker. By 2000 this figure had increased to an average of 310 times more. The average compensation package is $13.1 million per year for the CEOs of the 365 largest American firms.

Employment Agreement between Global Crossing Ltd. and Robert Annunziata
(Excerpt)

3. Salary; Signing Bonus; Loan. (a) Executive shall receive a salary of $500,000 per annum during the first three (3) years of the Term. Executive's salary shall be reviewed at least annually and may be increased but not decreased. . . .
(b) Within 10 days from the date of commencement of Executive's employment with the Company, the Company shall pay to Executive a $10 million signing bonus, payable in cash. . . .
(c) The Company shall make available a full recourse unsecured loan facility to Executive at the commencement of Executive's employment with the Company in an aggregate principal amount not to exceed $5 million in order to allow Executive to purchase shares of the Company's common stock. . . .

4. Annual Bonus. For each year of the Term, Executive will be eligible for an annual bonus which will be determined by the Board of Directors, but which shall not be less than $500,000 for any year during the Term. The bonus shall be reviewed at least annually by the Board of Directors and may be increased but not decreased.

5. Stock Options. Subject to Board approval, Executive shall be granted stock options (the "Two Million Options") to purchase an aggregate of Two Million (2,000,000) shares of common stock of the Company. . . .

7. Benefits. Executive shall be entitled to receive the following benefits:
(a) Health care coverage equivalent to that provided to the Company's other executive officers.
(b) Reimbursement of reasonable living expenses for temporary housing in the Los Angeles area until permanent accommodations are arranged but not later than December 31, 1999, and reimbursement of reasonable relocation expenses.
(c) Monthly First Class airfare to Los Angeles for members of Executive's immediate family (spouse, mother and all children including the child of his wife, Patricia).
(d) Private aircraft, if available, or First Class airfare and limousine service to/from residence and/or office in connection with all company travel and for appropriate trips to New Jersey until permanent living arrangements are made in Los Angeles as required. . . .
(e) Four (4) weeks paid vacation each year during the Term.

Source: The Corporate Library, http://www.thecorporatelibrary.com (January 1, 2003).

Shareholders' rights activist Nell Minnow cites Robert Annunziata's contract with Global Crossing as an example of bad corporate governance because his salary and perks are not tied to performance. CEO contracts are public documents, and Minnow has posted many on www.corporatelibrary.com.

Ratio of CEO to Average Worker Pay 1965 to 2000	
1965	26.0
1978	36.5
1989	71.7
1998	256.0
2000	310.0

Source: Economic Policy Institute.

In 35 years, the average CEO went from earning 26 times more than the average worker to earning 310 times more.

In March 2002 six former attorneys for Enron are sworn in before testifying to the House Energy and Commerce Committee about the collapse of the former energy giant.

During the 1990s, compensation committees increasingly relied on stock options as a way to retain talented managers. Stock options grant employees the right to purchase shares of company stock for a set price in a set period of time, usually several years. The price is often set at or above the current price of the stock. These options give employees an incentive to work hard because improving company performance will increase the price of the stock and raise the value of the options. Stock options were especially popular during the dot-com boom of the 1990s, when many companies were underfunded but needed to attract top talent to turn a profit. In essence, stock options offered employees tremendous wealth if the company succeeded.

Stock options also give management an incentive to take actions that increase the value of the stock. For example, if a CEO has been granted one million options to buy stock at $20 and the price of the stock increases to $30, she could realize $10 million if she exercised the options. Managers lose nothing if the stock price falls, as they are not required to exercise the option. As options became more common and increasingly generous, the temptation intensified for CEOs to use less-than-legitimate means to drive up the price of their company's stock.

Another important question about stock options is how they are reported in financial documents. Accountants have a difficult time identifying the cost of stock options because they may or may not be used. Formerly, accounting standards did not require companies to report the value of their options. This reduced the projected future expenses of these companies and made them appear more prosperous. The legislative response to the accounting scandals of 2001–2002 is likely to lead to changes in how options are reported.

Corporate Scandals

The trends of weak corporate governance and the spread of stock options coincided with changes in the investment banking and accounting industries. Banking and

accounting firms audit corporate balance sheets and provide investors with outside assessments of corporate performance. During the 1990s many of these companies merged and started providing both accounting and consulting services, creating incentives to curry management's favor through friendly accounting evaluations in hopes of gaining consulting business. In some cases, the so-called outside assessments were adjusted according to the wishes of management.

The temptation to inflate stock prices, combined with weak corporate governance and reduced accounting rigor, culminated in a series of corporate scandals, bankruptcies, and a crisis in confidence in corporate America during 2002. Executives from several major corporations, including Enron, Adelphia (see sidebar), and WorldCom, were accused of crimes ranging from embezzlement to fraud and racketeering. These accusations and indictments contributed to a pronounced slump in the stock market as investors worldwide lost confidence in management and corporate leadership.

The scandals of 2002 typically featured something called off-balance-sheet loans—corporations either directly lending officers money or guaranteeing their loans to banks. These sums, which often ranged into the tens of millions of dollars, were lent without the knowledge of the stockholders.

In 2002 Congress and the president acted with unusual speed to initiate a number of reforms aimed at restoring investor trust. These included imposing stiffer penalties for executive mismanagement and requiring that CEOs personally vouch for the accuracy of accounting statements. The efficacy of these reforms has not yet been proven.

Stockholders are also taking an active interest in corporate reform. Large investors, including pension boards and mutual funds, are pressuring corporations to explicitly include stock options on their balance sheets. Many institutions, because of their large investments, have taken the position that they are not just stockholders but stakeholders, or active participants, in corporate decisions.

Adelphia Communications

John Rigas started Adelphia Communications in 1952 and built it into one of the nation's largest cable television companies. Its stock price peaked at $33 per share in January 2002. Adelphia appeared to be a strong investment because of its broad subscriber base and solid finances.

The Rigas family maintained control of the company by owning the majority of the outstanding stock with voting rights. Both of John's sons held important positions in the company: Timothy served as chief financial officer and Michael as executive vice president of operations.

Public perception of Adelphia changed dramatically as the result of a conference call with stock analysts in March 2002. Company officials were unable to give satisfactory answers about why the company had made and failed to disclose $2.3 billion of loans to the Rigas family.

By July prosecutors were convinced that Adelphia was not simply being mismanaged. John Rigas was arrested on a number of charges, including fraud and racketeering. The criminal complaint alleged that former executives improperly took company funds for personal use, including vacations and the construction of a private golf course on family property.

The financial health of the company was placed in serious jeopardy. Adelphia declared bankruptcy in 2002 to gain protection from its creditors and plans to borrow more than $1 billion to remain in operation. Adelphia's major assets are cable television subscribers, and the company may be forced to sell tens of thousands of accounts to competitors to stay in business.

Businesspeople must take risks to generate profits, and they risk losing out to competition if supervision and controls are too stringent. Policy makers will attempt to find a balance that restores investor confidence while minimizing economic losses from regulation. This illustrates the core conundrum of capitalism: how to best focus greed toward productive ends while limiting its excesses.

Further Reading

Blair, Margaret M., and Bruce MacLaury. *Ownership and Control: Rethinking Corporate Governance for the 21st Century.* Washington, D.C.: Brookings Institute, 1995.

Dimsdale, Nicholas, and Margaret Prevezer. *Capital Markets and Corporate Governance.* Oxford: Clarendon Press; New York: Oxford University Press, 1994.

The Harvard Business Review on Corporate Governance. Boston: Harvard Business School Press, 2000.

Monks, Robert A., and Nell Minnow, eds. *Corporate Governance.* 2nd ed. Malden, Mass.: Blackwell Publishing, 2001.

Ward, Ralph D. *Improving Corporate Boards: The Boardroom Insider Guidebook.* New York: John Wiley & Sons, 2000.

—*David Long*

Corporate Social Responsibility

Accompanying U.S. industrial development in the 1900s was a growing anxiety about the harmful effects of some business practices. Public concern throughout the century produced a laundry list of business infractions, many too serious to be ignored. Corporations responded to public pressure and government interventions with an increasing sense of social responsibility. Development of corporate social responsibility followed an uneven track throughout the twentieth century.

In the late 1800s and early 1900s, when the labor supply was plentiful, powerful industry owners realized large profits by paying workers poorly and not spending money to make workplaces safe. In this era, the general American view of businessmen was highly negative. Businessmen appeared to be interested only in profits for themselves and had little concern for the welfare of workers. One exception was businessman George Pullman. He proactively addressed the needs of his industrial workers (who built Pullman Palace railway cars) by establishing Pullman Town, just south of Chicago, between the 1870s and 1880s. This "company town" was intended to control the workers by forcing them to be moral and upright citizens, but Pullman also furnished housing, schools, and parks (which other company towns did not), and stores (which other company towns did, but with higher

The magazine Business Ethics *ranks socially responsible companies using a variety of criteria, including environmental responsibility, diversity in the workplace, and the quality of employee, customer, and community relations.*

Top 100 Corporate Citizens of 2002: Rated by *Business Ethics*

Rank	Company	Rank	Company	Rank	Company	Rank	Company
1.	IBM	26.	Freddie Mac	51.	Eastman Kodak	76.	Rouse Company
2.	Hewlett-Packard	27.	J. P. Morgan Chase	52.	Tennant Co.	77.	Nordson Corp.
3.	Fannie Mae	28.	Adolph Coors	53.	Eli Lilly and Co.	78.	Tektronix
4.	St. Paul Companies	29.	Whirlpool	54.	Northwest Natural Gas	79.	CIGNA Corp.
5.	Procter & Gamble	30.	Tellabs	55.	Merix Corp.	80.	Charles Schwab
6.	Motorola, Inc.	31.	Corning, Inc.	56.	Network Appliance	81.	Energen
7.	Cummins Engine	32.	Medtronic, Inc.	57.	Nucor	82.	Guidant
8.	Herman Miller	33.	Cisco Systems	58.	Sonoco Products	83.	PNC Financial Services
9.	General Mills, Inc.	34.	3M	59.	Wells Fargo	84.	Oracle Corp.
10.	Avon Products	35.	Pitney Bowes	60.	MBNA Corp.	85.	Analog Devices
11.	Intel Corp.	36.	AT&T	61.	Clorox	86.	Oxford Health Plans
12.	State Street Corp.	37.	American Express	62.	Modine Manufacturing	87.	McDonald's
13.	H. B. Fuller	38.	Gillette	63.	Home Depot	88.	Graco
14.	Timberland	39.	Symantec Corp.	64.	Deere & Co.	89.	Marriott International
15.	Bank of America	40.	Baxter International	65.	New York Times	90.	Xilinx
16.	Amgen	41.	Merck & Co.	66.	Peoplesoft	91.	MBIA, Inc.
17.	Lucent Technologies	42.	Solectron, Inc.	67.	Arrow Electronics	92.	Washington Gas & Light
18.	Qualcomm	43.	Golden West Financial	68.	Autodesk	93.	Safeco
19.	Sun Microsystems	44.	Scholastic Corp.	69.	Apache	94.	Emerson Electric
20.	Southwest Airlines	45.	Oneok	70.	Delphi Automotive	95.	PPG Industries
21.	Starbucks	46.	3Com Corp.	71.	Microsoft	96.	Adobe Systems
22.	Fed Ex Corp.	47.	Lexmark International	72.	Harman International	97.	Wendy's International
23.	Brady Corp.	48.	Compaq Computer	73.	Devry, Inc.	98.	Tribune Company
24.	Northern Trust Corp.	49.	Ecolab	74.	FirstFed Financial	99.	Kroger
25.	UnumProvident	50.	Texas Instruments	75.	Airproducts & Chemicals	100.	Applied Materials

Source: Business Ethics. Used with permission.

prices). However, his goal of avoiding strikes was defeated in 1894 when his workers rebelled against not only their reduced pay but also the interference of the corporation in their daily lives.

The concept of corporate responsibility to workers emerged again in the 1910s and 1920s with the development of "business welfare capitalism." Hundreds of firms established social support systems for their workers, including pensions, profit-sharing plans, health care, adult education, and so on. Many of these programs extolled the virtues of American society (and thus this movement was also known as the Americanization movement) and featured experiments in democratic governance in the workplace. Henry Ford had been a major contributor to this movement in the mid-1910s when he raised wages and established the so-called $5 day. As had Pullman, Ford interfered heavily in the everyday affairs of his workers. To earn the $5, workers had to work much harder than before and allow Ford's "social workers" access to their homes to confirm that they were living moral lives.

At the same time, American business leaders began to establish programs to encourage a greater sense of business responsibility to society. This included expanding business education in universities and colleges and having executives join local philanthropic and service organizations (for example, the Rotary and Kiwanis clubs). These movements were clear attempts to move away from the negative stereotype of businessmen that had developed in the late nineteenth century.

Much of the progress made in the 1920s toward more socially responsible business practices was undermined by the financial strains of the Great Depression. The Depression also led Americans to view business less favorably and built sympathy for unions. The New Deal established the Fair Labor Standards Act to force businesses to pay higher wages (not all workers were covered; women and tenant farmers were omitted initially).

In the boom years of the 1950s corporate responsibility to workers and society emerged

Web Resources on Corporate Social Responsibility

www.worldcsr.com/pages is a collection of links to Web sites of the leading international organizations concerned with corporate social responsibility.

www.csrforum.com, the Corporate Social Responsibility Forum, promotes responsible business practices.

www.bsr.org is the Web site of a global nonprofit organization that offers resources to its member companies to promote ethical values and responsible business practices.

www.csrwire.com is a newswire service that provides press releases and reports that promote corporate social responsibility.

www.csramericas.org is the Web site of a consortium of North and South American companies that implement corporate social responsibility programs and initiatives.

again as a coherent movement. Invoking "duty to the employee," corporations expanded the older welfare capitalism programs of the 1920s. In addition to pensions, profit sharing, and improved health plans, employers offered programs for spouses and children of the male workers. Civic programs, abandoned in the Depression, also reemerged to reflect a new sense of "duty to society." These measures, generous as they may have been, also had a clear economic motive: to engender employee and consumer loyalty to the firm.

Broadening Responsibility

For most of the twentieth century, corporations had little or no inclination to act for the public good, as opposed to the good of their employees. The modern environmental movement, greatly inspired by Rachel Carson's book *Silent Spring* (1962), emerged in the 1960s and 1970s to challenge corporate behavior on a broad public level. Environmentalists argued that certain kinds of consumption and waste production are disproportionately harmful and that some industries acted recklessly, promoting and profiting from practices that were essentially destroying ecological systems.

From the environmental movement, pressure grew on corporations to take social responsibility for the condition of the Earth, the air, the water, and life itself. Activists devoted to land issues questioned mining practices and land pollution and pushed for recycling to slow landfill development and resource depletion. Others raised concerns about the dangers of certain kinds of energy production and hazardous waste. Scientists were enlisted to study air quality, to evaluate ozone depletion, global warming, and the levels and effects of air pollution. In nearly every instance, corporate practices were called into question and industries were asked to be accountable.

At about the same time, profound social changes forced corporations to reconsider issues of equity in the workplace. Minorities and women argued that because of discriminatory practices, they were being paid less for equal work and were overlooked for promotions that went to less-qualified white males. Again, interest groups put business under fire.

Industry, facing mounting public pressure but heavily invested in the status quo, clung to established practices. Corporate powers argued that equity problems were overstated and that addressing environmental issues would compromise profitability. The impasse between activist insistence and industrial resistance forced the government to take action in the public interest.

Between 1969 and 1972, some of the most important business-related social legislation in U.S. history was passed. Four regulatory agencies were established, all greatly affecting American business: the Environmental Protection Agency (EPA), the Occupational Safety and Health Administration (OSHA), the Equal Employment Opportunity Commission (EEOC), and the Consumer Product Safety Commission (CPSC). The majority of businesses were caught unawares by the social legislation of the 1960s, for example, the Civil Rights Act of 1964. Many businesses established Political Action Committees (PACs) to combat expansion of these programs, but met with little success.

The election of Ronald Reagan to the presidency in 1980 shifted Washington's agenda. With increased concern for corporate independence and profits, the federal government vowed to intrude less in business affairs. Several times, the administration attempted to repeal the social legislation of the previous decade.

Although the 1980s tend to be remembered as a pro-business, pro-greed era, a watershed in the history of corporate social responsibility occurred in 1982, after seven people were killed by cyanide-laced Tylenol capsules. Johnson & Johnson, producers of the over-the-counter pain reliever, reacted quickly, making the public aware of the tampering and recalling millions of bottles of the drug at a cost of more than $100 million. At the time, industry experts believed that Johnson & Johnson was doomed, but the company's swift and forthright handling of the crisis improved the company's reputation rather than destroying it.

On March 24, 1989, an Exxon oil tanker ran aground in the icy waters of Alaska's Prince William Sound, spilling 11 million gallons of crude oil along more than one thousand miles of previously pristine shoreline. The world watched vivid and disturbing broadcasts of Exxon workers and volunteers swabbing gummy black oil from the wings of gasping sea birds, while Exxon executives appeared to be reluctant to take responsibility for the disaster. That oil spill, as well as the earlier toxic discoveries at Love Canal in the early 1970s and the Three Mile Island nuclear accident in 1979, renewed public outrage at

In 1986 Johnson & Johnson president David Clare testifies before a U.S. Senate hearing about tamperproof packaging. Most analysts believe that Johnson & Johnson's forthright handling of the product-tampering tragedy in 1982 saved the company from ruin.

the lack of corporate concern for people and the environment.

Responsibility versus Profit?

Throughout the twentieth century, many businesses came to realize that irresponsible corporate behavior was not only publicly unacceptable but also economically imprudent. The high cost of fighting government regulation together with the damaging effects of public criticism adversely affected profits. Honest and ethical business leaders in the United States and throughout the world sought to distance themselves from scandalous business activity. In developing a proactive stance on the public issues that are part of corporate concern, these business leaders paved the way for voluntary corporate social responsibility.

The earliest form of a voluntary corporate citizenry was philanthropic. What began as donations to charity expanded to include extensive involvement in workers' communities. Most major corporations added a section to their annual reports detailing their community involvement. Time Warner, for example, issued a special report entitled *Community Connections* discussing its involvement in education and literacy, its support of the arts, its promotion of diversity, and the volunteer activities of its employees.

Globalization provided enormous opportunities for industry in the late twentieth century. Corporations formed conglomerates, which supplied a number of new jobs and brought additional wealth to the countries where they operated. With worldwide operations and impact, businesses face broader ethical challenges and need to set a new agenda for corporate responsibility.

Corporate social responsibility, in its broadest sense, implies that corporations have stakeholder interest at a level equal to shareholder interest. In other words, profits should not occur at the expense of anyone or anything affected by the way a corporation conducts its business. Stakeholders include employees, customers, suppliers, community organizations, subsidiaries and affiliates, joint venture partners, local neighborhoods, and the environment. Common wisdom says that

Socially Responsible Investing: Domini 400 Social℠ Index (DSI) vs. Standard and Poor's 500
(total return as of 2002)

	DSI 400	S&P 500
One Year	–17.43%	–17.99%
Three Year *	–11.13%	–10.30%
Five Year *	2.61%	1.77%
Ten Year *	11.36%	10.40%

* Annualized returns.
Source: The Domini 400 Social℠ Index, DSI Performance Statistics, http://www.kld.com/benchmarks/dsi.html (September 20, 2002).

The Domini 400 Social℠ Index (DSI) is a benchmark that gauges the stock market performance of shares most socially responsible investors will buy. The DSI compares favorably with the traditonal Standard and Poor's 500.

when companies foster mutually beneficial relationships with stakeholders, they create sustainable communities that, in turn, will be supportive of business. When stakeholders are happy and live well, they form healthy communities that generate stable economies. All this is good for business in the long run.

By the late twentieth century, companies began to realize the benefits of this kind of responsibility. Research in the United States and Canada has shown that over time the most socially responsible companies become the most profitable. Furthermore, they are more likely to have their stock bought by investors. Most major families of mutual funds now have a category for socially responsible investing (SRI). These SRI funds are performing as well and sometimes better than the average mutual fund; as of 1999, $2.16 trillion had been invested in funds that adhered to a socially responsible investment ethic.

Further Reading

Bradshaw, Thornton, and David Vogel, eds. *Corporations and Their Critics: Issues and Answers to the Problems of Corporate Social Responsibility.* New York: McGraw-Hill, 1981.

Hawken, Paul. *The Ecology of Commerce: A Declaration of Sustainability.* New York: HarperBusiness, 1993.

McDonough, William, and Michael Braungart. "The NEXT Industrial Revolution." *The Atlantic Monthly,* October 1998. http://www.theatlantic.com/issues/98oct/industry.htm (January 2, 2003).

Monks, Robert A., and Nell Minnow, eds. *Corporate Governance.* 2nd ed. Malden, Mass.: Blackwell Publishing, 2001.

—*Karen Ehrle*

Corporation

In law, a corporation is an organization that is formed by a group of people for the purpose of carrying out certain specified activities and that is legally endowed with certain rights and duties. Corporations take various forms. A corporation may, for example, be a religious body (the word *incorporate* comes from the Roman Catholic church's medieval definition of itself as a "corpus") or it may be a municipal body. In the United States, government entities below the level of a state, for example, cities and counties, are considered to be corporations; the federal government itself has established corporations like the Community Credit Corporation and the Federal Deposit Insurance Corporation. A corporation may also be a charitable, nonprofit organization, or it may be what is known as a professional corporation, which can have only one stockholder (a licensed professional, like a doctor or engineer).

Most commonly, however, the corporation is thought of as a private association organized for the purpose of making a profit—a business. Legally, in the United States, a corporation is considered to be a person, a definition codified in the important Supreme Court decision of 1886, *Santa Clara County v. Southern Pacific Railroad*. In this case the Court ruled that, as a person, a corporation had the same rights as human individuals under the 1st Amendment and, especially, under the 14th Amendment, which states that "no state shall deprive any person of life, liberty, or property, without due process of law." As a person, a corporation can buy, sell, and own property, bring lawsuits, and enter into contracts. It also pays taxes and it can be prosecuted for crimes.

Unlike a person, a corporation can exist indefinitely. As Chief Justice John Marshall wrote in 1819, "a perpetual succession of individuals are capable of acting for the promotion of the particular object, like one immortal being." One of the chief advantages of a corporation is that it protects its owners (the shareholders) from unlimited, personal liability. In most instances, if a corporation cannot pay its debts, its assets may be seized and sold. However, the personal assets of the shareholders may not.

Historians trace the origin of corporations to antiquity, but their modern history is usually said to begin in the sixteenth century. Some of the best-known examples of early corporations were British overseas trading companies, including the Massachusetts Bay Company and the Hudson's Bay Company; both were joint-stock companies and, as such, are considered to be forerunners of the modern corporation.

Starting a Corporation

In the United States before the Industrial Revolution, corporations were individually granted by the special act of a state legislature. Eventually, state legislatures were empowered to authorize incorporation by general law, which enables a group of individuals to organize a corporation under "articles of incorporation," a document that is submitted for approval to a specific official, normally the state's secretary of state.

A corporation gains its initial financing from the sale of stock (shares). Small corporations are often owned by family or friends, or both, and their shares in stock are not publicly sold (a closed corporation). When very large financing is needed and a corporation's shares are publicly sold, the raising of capital is commonly the task of a promoter. Publicly sold companies often seek to incorporate in a state that has liberal incorporation laws—that is, with regulations less stringent in protecting investors' interests.

Corporations usually issue common or preferred shares. Holders of common stock are usually entitled to vote at the corporation's yearly meeting and receive dividends when the company declares them. Holders of preferred stock normally do not have voting rights but have precedence over owners of common stock in claiming dividends and assets. They also receive an annual dividend payment regardless of the corporation's profitability.

In addition to selling shares to raise capital, a corporation can be financed through borrowing. Corporations that have successfully conducted business for a while also have retained earnings that can be used as a source of financing for further business ventures.

Corporate Structure

As a rule, management of a corporation is divided into three groups: directors, officers, and shareholders. The directors are elected by the shareholders; they are charged with developing the corporation's policies and managing its affairs. Directors are also

Corporations: Selected Financial Items 1980 to 1998
(in billion dollars)

	1980	1990	1992	1994	1996	1998
No. of tax returns (in thousands)	2,711	3,717	3,869	4,342	4,631	4,849
Assets						
Cash	529	771	806	853	1,097	1,336
Notes and accounts receivable	1,985	4,198	4,169	4,768	5,783	7,062
Inventories	535	894	915	1,126	1,079	1,139
Investments in gov't. obligations	266	921	1,248	1,309	1,339	1,366
Mortgage and real estate	894	1,538	1,567	1,661	1,825	2,414
Other investments	1,214	4,137	4,971	6,265	8,657	13,201
Depreciable assets	2,107	4,318	4,755	5,284	5,923	6,541
Depletable assets	72	129	131	148	169	193
Land	93	210	221	239	254	271
Total[1]	7,617	18,190	20,002	23,446	28,642	37,347
Liabilities						
Accounts payable	542	1,094	1,605	1,606	1,905	2,501
Short-term debt[2]	505	1,803	1,560	1,831	2,328	3,216
Long-term debt[3]	987	2,665	2,742	3,100	3,651	4,813
Capital stock	417	1,585	1,881	2,132	2,278	3,244
Total[1]	7,617	18,190	20,002	23,446	28,642	37,347
Net worth	1,944	4,739	5,700	7,031	9,495	13,108
Receipts						
Business receipts	5,732	9,860	10,360	11,884	13,659	15,010
Interest	367	977	829	882	1,082	1,277
Rents and royalties	54	133	140	132	156	200
Total[1]	6,361	11,410	11,742	13,360	15,526	17,324
Deductions						
Costs of sales and operations	4,205	6,611	6,772	7,625	8,707	9,362
Compensation of officers	109	205	221	282	319	357
Rent paid on business property	72	185	196	223	248	308
Taxes paid	163	251	274	322	341	355
Interest paid	345	825	597	611	771	967
Depreciation	157	333	346	403	474	542
Advertising	52	126	134	157	177	198
Total[1]	6,125	11,033	11,330	12,775	14,728	16,489
Net income	297	553	570	740	987	1,091
Loss	58	182	168	162	180	253
Net income less loss	239	371	402	577	806	838

[1] Includes items not shown separately. [2] Payable in less than 1 year. [3] Payable in 1 year or more.
Source: U.S. Internal Revenue Service, *Statistics of Income: Corporation Income Tax Returns*, Washington, D.C.

Corporations by Size and Industry: By Receipts Class 1998
(Number in thousands; receipts in billion dollars)

Industry		Total	Under $1 mil.[1]	$1–$4.9 million	$5–$9.9 million	$10–$49.9 million	$50 mil. or more
Agriculture, forestry, fishing, and hunting	Number	135	120	12	2	1	(Z)
	Total receipts	100	20	25	11	19	25
Mining	Number	31	27	3	1	1	(Z)
	Total receipts	117	4	7	4	12	90
Utilities	Number	8	7	1	(Z)	(Z)	(Z)
	Total receipts	451	1	1	1	4	443
Construction	Number	552	420	102	16	111	1
	Total receipts	859	103	220	111	213	213
Manufacturing	Number	310	192	75	18	19	6
	Total receipts	4,591	52	174	125	389	3,851
Wholesale and retail trade	Number	957	657	213	39	40	8
	Total receipts	4,517	180	462	270	842	2,763
Transportation and warehousing	Number	160	129	23	4	3	1
	Total receipts	470	24	50	26	55	315
Information	Number	101	85	12	2	2	1
	Total receipts	668	14	24	14	38	578
Finance and insurance	Number	218	183	21	5	6	3
	Total receipts	2,358	29	48	33	128	2,119
Real estate, rental, and leasing	Number	522	500	19	2	1	(Z)
	Total receipts	176	14	38	12	22	63
Professional, scientific, and technical services	Number	624	557	54	8	5	1
	Total receipts	541	97	108	53	95	188
Educational services	Number	37	33	3	1	(Z)	(Z)
	Total receipts	23	5	5	5	3	5
Health care and social services	Number	307	260	39	5	3	(Z)
	Total receipts	357	73	75	33	49	126
Arts, entertainment, and recreation	Number	93	85	7	1	(Z)	(Z)
	Total receipts	60	15	13	4	7	20
Accommodation and food services	Number	245	211	31	2	1	(Z)
	Total receipts	296	54	58	16	25	143
Other services	Number	300	277	21	1	1	(Z)
	Total receipts	143	55	39	7	15	27
Total[2]	Number	4,849	3,956	661	110	98	24
	Receipts	16,543	805	1,403	763	1,978	11,594

[1] Includes businesses without receipts. [2] Includes businesses not allocable to individual industries.
Notes: (Z) = fewer than 500 returns. Figures are estimates based on a sample of unaudited tax returns.
Source: U.S. Internal Revenue Service, *Statistics of Income,* various publications, and unpublished data.

responsible for deciding when to declare dividends. Directors do not, however, conduct the day-to-day operations of the corporation, a job that falls to the officers (although in most U.S. states, the corporation's president is required to be one of the directors).

The officers of the corporation usually include the chief executive officer, the chief financial officer, and the treasurer. Although shareholders commonly have the right to vote at company meetings, in some cases voting rights are limited or nonexistent. In practice, most shareholder voting is done by proxy (the shareholder designates in writing someone to vote in his or her place).

Although Marshall described a corporation as "immortal," its lifetime can be limited for several reasons. Some corporations are intended from the beginning to have a limited lifetime—when the term laid out in the

Corporate Profits before Taxes by Industry
1990 to 1999
(in million dollars)

	1990	1993	1994	1995	1996	1997	1998	1999
Agriculture, forestry, and fishing	1,638	1,911	1,385	1,842	2,950	3,059	3,104	4,355
Mining	2,502	1,509	3,348	4,517	8,124	10,972	3,184	2,376
Construction	10,922	10,148	13,650	17,265	21,932	25,696	32,758	36,229
Manufacturing	113,552	107,711	144,709	172,518	175,789	192,312	167,600	183,909
Transportation	954	6,368	10,316	11,613	16,157	18,639	22,148	24,470
Communications	20,049	33,202	36,837	33,604	35,012	25,570	22,966	26,641
Electric, gas, and sanitary services	24,928	29,730	35,801	40,677	40,854	39,782	37,418	38,589
Wholesale trade	21,201	30,614	36,883	35,546	41,588	46,315	50,905	58,455
Retail trade	24,896	41,831	49,187	47,471	54,806	62,648	76,512	84,784
Finance, insurance, and real estate	88,334	129,104	117,726	106,062	171,827	195,658	180,922	190,752
Services	19,836	41,506	46,326	51,327	56,453	61,055	57,155	61,000

Source: U.S. Bureau of Economic Analysis, *National Income and Product Accounts of the United States, 1929–97*, and *Survey of Current Business*, Washington, D.C., July 2001.

articles of incorporation is reached, the company's dissolution is automatic. A corporation may also be dissolved by a vote of the shareholders (a voluntary dissolution); another form of voluntary dissolution occurs when the corporation is merged into another (as opposed to a consolidation, in which each of the combining companies continues to exist).

A dissolution can also be involuntary—a minority of the shareholders, if they believe the company is being mismanaged, can bring a lawsuit seeking the termination of the corporation. Another kind of involuntary dissolution occurs when a bankrupt company is sued by its creditors or when the state acts to dissolve the corporation in response to corporate misconduct or a failure to pay taxes. When a corporation is dissolved, it gathers its assets, pays its debts (as best it can), and distributes its remaining resources to the shareholders.

Multinationals

Perhaps the most significant development for the corporate form is the rise of the international, or multinational, corporation. Beginning in the late nineteenth century, faster transportation and a desire to expand markets—combined with companies' needs for items found overseas, like oil and minerals—permitted, or even compelled, companies to expand beyond the borders of the nations in which they were founded.

Multinational corporations normally have a parent company, located in the country of the firm's origin, and various subsidiaries in other nations. Sometimes these subsidiaries have a different name from the parent company, and the amount of direct control exercised by the parent can vary. When a corporation becomes a multinational, its goals and strategies no longer apply to one country but become regional or global.

A 1995 United Nations survey counted 40,000 multinational corporations in the world with approximately 250,000 foreign affiliates; in 1993 the *Economist* magazine estimated that the 300 biggest multinational corporations controlled about one-fourth of the world's productive assets.

Analysts often point out that the annual sales of some of the biggest multinationals exceed the gross domestic product of many individual countries.

Public Opinion of Corporations

Surveys indicate that the U.S. public is of two minds about corporations and corporate power. A poll taken by *BusinessWeek* magazine in August 2000 showed that although two-thirds of respondents praised U.S. corporations for making good products and being globally competitive, no fewer than three-quarters of them said that big business had gained too much power over their lives. Several factors were cited for the unpopularity of corporations, including a declining standard of customer service, the failure of wages and benefits to keep pace with productivity increases, burnout and mandatory overtime among employees, and, perhaps most of all, excessive executive pay.

The bankruptcies of the Enron Corporation (2001) and WorldCom (2002) and subsequent revelations of widespread unethical business practices served only to heighten the suspicion of corporations among the U.S. public. Taking a long-term view, however, some analysts pointed out that, although corporations might be entering the twenty-first century with a generally unenviable image, the U.S. public's good opinion of corporations has waxed and waned throughout history.

Further Reading

Beatty, Jack, ed. *Colossus: How the Corporation Changed America.* New York: Broadway Books, 2001.

Blackford, Mansel G., and K. Austin Kerr. *Business Enterprise in American History.* 3rd ed. Boston: Houghton Mifflin, 1994.

Boyce, Gordon, and Simon Ville. *The Development of Modern Business.* New York: Palgrave, 2002.

Roy, William G. *Socializing Capital: The Rise of the Large Industrial Corporation in America.* Princeton, N.J.: Princeton University Press, 1997.

Sobel, Robert. *The Age of Giant Corporations: A Microeconomic History of American Business, 1914–1992.* 3rd ed. Westport, Conn.: Greenwood Press, 1993.

—Joseph Gustaitis

Cost

Cost is a deceptively simple-sounding term and can have different meanings in different decision-making contexts. In order to make sound choices, it is crucial to understand the nature of different types of cost.

What Is Cost?

Cost can refer to an amount of money paid to acquire a good or service. Alternatively, if a purchaser agrees to pay for the good or service in the future, the cost is the amount of the debt. Some transactions do not involve cash; in transactions wherein a purchaser acquires a good or service by giving up another asset, the cost is the value of the asset exchanged. In short, a general definition of cost is the amount given up or forgone to acquire a good or service. Most people use various kinds of cost information in decisions they make every day.

Cost is related to, but not the same as, expense. An expense is how much of an asset or service is consumed or used during a specific period. For example, assume a driver buys an old automobile for $2,000 cash and it lasts for two years. The cost of the automobile is $2,000 because that is the amount of cash paid in exchange for it. However, the yearly expense is $1,000, because that is the amount of the cost consumed (or expired) during each year of the automobile's two-year life.

Cost is related to, but not the same as, value. One way to measure value is to determine the amount that an asset or service can be sold for. For example, assume the owner of the automobile who has purchased it for $2,000 decides to sell it six months after purchase. The best offer is $1,200. The value may have changed but the cost is still $2,000, the amount of money originally paid for the automobile.

Why Are Costs Important?

Costs are important to businesses and consumers. Businesses must know the cost of

See also:
Budget; Opportunity Cost; Profit and Loss.

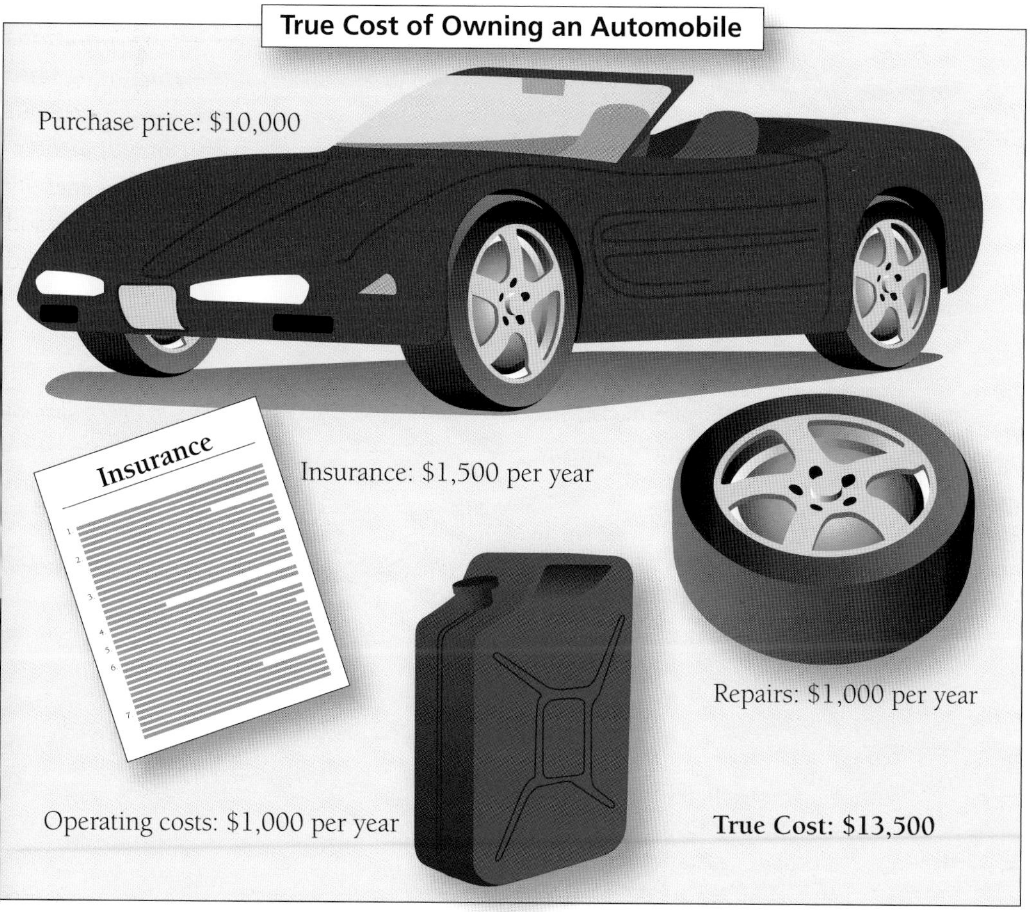

True Cost of Owning an Automobile

Purchase price: $10,000

Insurance: $1,500 per year

Repairs: $1,000 per year

Operating costs: $1,000 per year

True Cost: $13,500

In analyzing costs, consider both the initial costs and the operating costs.

running the organization to establish sales prices that both cover costs and generate a profit. Businesses also need to know how costs are likely to change when making certain decisions. For example, if the owner of a hardware store decides to open a second store, additional costs will be incurred. Such costs include salaries, electricity, rent, and the price of merchandise to be sold.

Consumers regularly use various kinds of cost information. Examples of decisions that use cost information are whether to rent or buy housing and whether to buy or lease an automobile. Cost is also important in everyday shopping decisions. For example, cost may be important in deciding what brand of cereal to buy in a grocery store. Of course, cost tradeoffs may be made because the cereal that tastes better and is more nutritious may cost more.

Cost information may be very important to buyers of automobiles. Costs that should be considered in such a decision include not only the initial purchase price but also operating expenses. For example, someone considering the purchase of a four-year-old automobile for $8,000 should also consider the yearly operating costs. Such costs include automobile insurance, gas and oil, and repairs.

Cost information is also useful in selecting a college to attend. Examples of costs that would be included in this decision are tuition, room and board, books and supplies, and commuting expenses. Scholarships, a kind of negative cost, would also be important as they would reduce the cost of a particular college. For example, if a very prestigious university has total costs of $25,000 per year but awards an applicant a $10,000 scholarship, the net cost would be $15,000. If a less prestigious university has total costs of $18,000 per year but does not award the applicant a scholarship, the more prestigious university is actually less costly by $3,000 per year.

Consumers analyze cost trade-offs every day; for example, a particular brand of cereal might be more expensive than another, but it also might be more nutritious or taste better.

Opportunity Costs

In some situations a student might forfeit income from employment to pursue another alternative. For example, if a student could work for $9 per hour but really enjoys playing soccer, the student may decide to forfeit income of $9 per hour to play soccer. The cost arises because the student gave up income to play soccer, even though the student did not have to pay any cash. Such costs are referred to as opportunity costs; these are costs because they have been forfeited or given up.

Other significant opportunity costs could be associated with going to college. For example, if a potential college student is able to secure a job paying $20,000 per year after graduation from high school and the costs of going to college are $14,000 per year, the total costs of going to college are $34,000 per year. In addition to the $14,000 the college student would pay the college, the college student is giving up income of $20,000 per year.

Of course, trade-offs exist in the decision of whether the student should go to college and which college should be selected. Going to college may lead to a higher quality of life, and the student may earn an increased salary over time as a result of having attended college. Also, even though a more prestigious college may be more costly than a less prestigious college, many intangible benefits may result from attending the more prestigious college. The quality of education may be better and job opportunities (in terms of quality and number) may be better. Such benefits are difficult to measure and include in a cost-benefit analysis.

Relevant Costs

In some situations a decision maker may wish to understand if his costs will change as

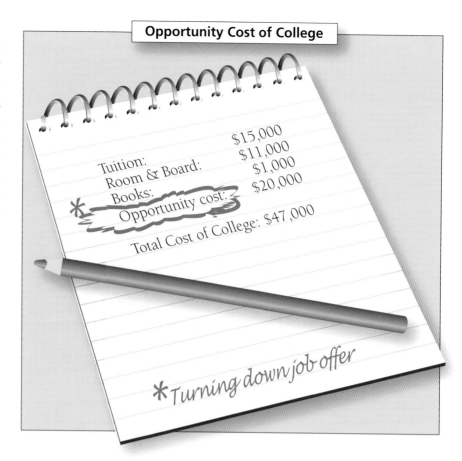

a result of selecting a particular course of action. Such costs are relevant costs; relevant costs can differ among the various alternatives being considered.

For example, assume a job seeker is considering two possible jobs. The two positions are similar in many respects: They both require a similar level of skill, and they both pay a similar amount. Both jobs are also the same distance from the job seeker's apartment. The job environments are different in one way. The workweek of one (Job A) is five eight-hour days while the workweek of the second (Job B) is four 10-hour days.

The job seeker is interested in knowing if living and commuting expenses are

Opportunity costs, or the cost of making one choice as opposed to another, should also be considered when making a decision.

Kinds of Costs: Purchasing a Car

Cost	Example
Relevant costs	Insurance
Negative costs	Manufacturer rebate
Opportunity costs	No money for DVD player
Sunk costs	Down payment

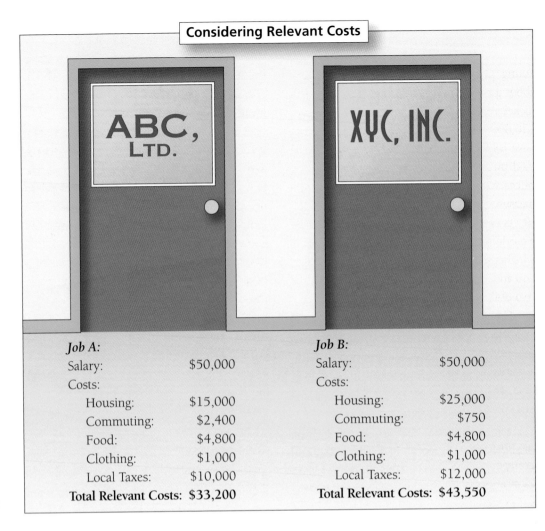

Considering Relevant Costs

Job A:		Job B:	
Salary:	$50,000	Salary:	$50,000
Costs:		Costs:	
Housing:	$15,000	Housing:	$25,000
Commuting:	$2,400	Commuting:	$750
Food:	$4,800	Food:	$4,800
Clothing:	$1,000	Clothing:	$1,000
Local Taxes:	$10,000	Local Taxes:	$12,000
Total Relevant Costs: $33,200		**Total Relevant Costs: $43,550**	

Although the salaries of the two jobs are the same, analyzing relevant costs might help the job seeker choose one over the other.

different for the two jobs. The job seeker's living expenses, like rent, food, and automobile payments, are going to be the same whichever job he accepts. However, commuting expenses are going to be higher for Job A, as it requires five trips per week while Job B requires only four. This difference in commuting costs may be the deciding factor in choosing one job over the other.

Sunk Costs

In some situations a cost resulting from a past decision is not important to a future decision. Such costs are referred to as "sunk" costs because they cannot be changed in the future.

Businesses sometimes make long-term commitments that are not easily changed. Costs resulting from such commitments are sunk; they cannot be changed in the short term. For example, assume a business commits to renting a building for the next 12-month period. At the end of the eighth month the business decides the building is no longer needed. Should the building be vacated? In analyzing this question, the cost of renting the building is a sunk cost; it will be incurred whether the business uses the building or vacates the building. The business must either accept this expense or find a way to make up the sunk cost—for example, by subletting the building to someone else.

Further Reading

Chadwick, Leslie. *The Essence of Management Accounting*. 2nd ed. Hertfordshire, England: Prentice Hall Europe, 1997.

Cooper, Robin, and Robert S. Kaplan. "Measure Costs Right: Make the Right Decisions." *Harvard Business Review* (September–October 1988), 97–98.

Solomons, David. *Studies in Cost Analysis*. 2nd ed. Homewood, Ill.: Richard D. Irwin, 1968.

—Donald W. Gribbin

Cost of Living

Young people often hear older people talk about the "good old days" when gasoline cost a nickel a gallon and new homes sold for under $20,000. Did people in previous generations have a higher standard of living because they paid prices that seem low compared with the prices we pay today? Absolute prices (prices measured simply in dollars, unadjusted for the effects of inflation or changes in income levels) were lower in the past. The real question is whether relative prices (prices adjusted for inflation and income) were lower. Economists use a cost-of-living index to answer this question.

Cost-of-living indexes are mechanisms for measuring and comparing how much income (or money) is needed to acquire a specific quantity of goods and services over a given time, or to achieve a certain standard of living in a specific country or area. Thus, cost of living compares income at a given time to average prices at a given time. For example, if, on average, a smaller percentage of a family's income is needed to buy a house today than the percentage needed to buy a house in an earlier time, the cost of living may be lower today than it was during the "good old days," even though houses cost more in absolute or unadjusted dollars.

Because cost of living is a ratio of average prices to average income level, it is closely linked to inflation (the changes in the average price of goods and services over time). The cost of living is often represented by a price index like the Consumer Price Index (CPI). The CPI in the United States has been compiled by the Bureau of Labor Statistics (BLS) since 1890. It measures the changing cost of a specific market basket of goods and services (a loaf of bread, a pair of jeans, and a movie ticket, for example) that many consumers need and purchase. An increase in the CPI indicates that the cost of this market basket of goods and services has increased, and so, too, has the cost of living (unless average incomes have increased at the same rate). Thus when the CPI rises, consumers tend to pay more.

Changes in the CPI are often used to determine cost-of-living adjustments (COLAs) to people's salaries and to other income payments. The BLS estimates that CPI-based COLAs affect the income of about 80 million individuals, including food stamp recipients, military and federal Civil Service retirees and survivors, and more than two million private-sector workers. In 2001, for example, 48.4 million Social Security beneficiaries received a CPI-based COLA.

Cost of living is also linked to the concept of purchasing power (the amount of goods and services that can be purchased with a given amount of money). Purchasing power declines as prices rise. Because rising inflation indicates higher prices, inflation leads to falling purchasing power. When purchasing

See also:
Consumer Price Index;
Inflation; Standard of Living.

Social Security payments include automatic benefit increases to adjust for increases in the cost of living. These increases, also known as cost-of-living adjustments (COLAs), have been in effect since 1975.

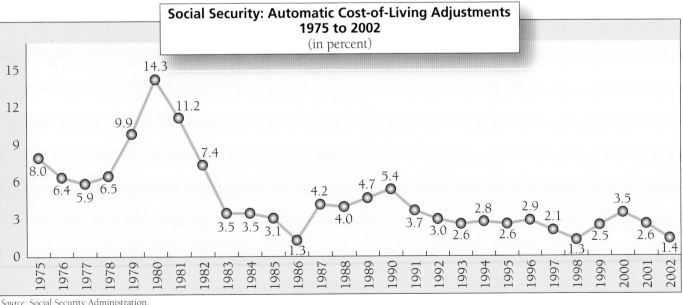

Social Security: Automatic Cost-of-Living Adjustments 1975 to 2002
(in percent)

Source: Social Security Administration.

Basket of Goods: 1930 versus 2001

Item	1930 retail price[1]	Hours of labor needed (1930)[2]	2001 retail price[3]	Hours of labor needed (2001)[4]	Percent change in retail price	Percent change in hours of labor needed
Men's wool suit with vest	$23.50	42.73	$169.99	10.88	623.36%	–74.55%
Men's leather oxford dress shoes	4.95	9.00	65.00	4.16	1213.13%	–53.79%
Set of golf clubs (3 woods, 9 irons)	32.85	59.73	199.00	12.73	505.78%	–78.68%
Living room set (sofa, two chairs)	130.70	237.64	1,199.00	76.71	817.37%	–67.72%
Refrigerator (18.5 cu. ft.)	45.25	82.27	449.95	28.79	894.36%	–65.01%
Upright vacuum cleaner (12 amps)	29.95	54.45	149.95	9.59	400.67%	–82.38%
Gallon interior paint (semi-gloss enamel)	2.70	4.91	16.99	1.09	529.26%	–77.86%
Bayer® aspirin (100 tablets)	.98	1.78	5.79	0.37	490.82%	–79.21%
Orange juice (48 oz.)	.59	1.07	2.59	0.17	338.98%	–84.55%
Extra-virgin olive oil (16 oz.)	.45	0.82	3.99	0.26	786.67%	–68.80%
Cookies (1 lb. box, assorted)	.29	0.53	3.39	0.22	1068.97%	–58.87%
Package of chewing gum	.03	0.05	.59	0.04	1866.67%	–30.80%
Box of chocolates (mixed)	.59	1.07	4.79	.31	711.86	–71.43%
Totals for basket	**$272.83**	**496.05**	**$2271.02**	**145.30**	**732.39%**	**–70.71%**

Notes: [1] 1930 retail prices taken from the 1930 Sears, Roebuck catalog. [2] Hours of labor—at 1930 average wage rate of $0.55/hour—needed to earn the retail price of item. [3] 2001 prices taken from Sears.com Web site or other similar retail outlet. [4] Hours of labor—at 2000 average wage rate of $15.36/hour—needed to earn the retail price of item.
Sources: U.S. Department of Labor Bureau of Labor Statistics, *National Compensation Survey: Occupational Wages in the United States, 1999,* Washington, D.C., 2001.
U.S. Department of Labor Bureau of Labor Statistics, *Employment, Hours, and Earnings: United States, 1909–1984,* Washington, D.C., 1985.

To assess changes in the cost of living from one year to the next, we need to compare prices for a similar basket of goods commonly purchased by a typical family. In the table, the prices for such a basket are compared for 1930 and 2001. Prices for goods in this particular basket were more than seven times higher in 2001 than they were for the same goods in 1930.

However, cost of living is a ratio of average prices to average income level. Therefore, to compare the cost of living in 2001 with that of 1930, we must also account for changes in the average income level over this time. According to the U.S. Bureau of Labor Statistics (2001), the average wage paid to workers in 1930 was

$0.55/hour. By 2000, the average wage had risen to $15.36/hour, a nearly 28-fold increase over 1930 wages.

In measuring the cost of living, changes in prices and changes in wages can be accounted for by determining the number of hours a worker would have to work to earn the income needed to purchase a specific good or service. Although the prices for the goods in this basket rose steeply between 1930 and 2001, the amount of work (in hours) needed to purchase the basket fell by more than two-thirds. Thus, despite price increases, U.S. consumers in 2001 can buy the same basket of goods for less effort than was required in 1930. The real cost of living has dropped.

power falls, the cost of living tends to rise: if one dollar buys less than it used to buy (has less purchasing power), then a consumer will need more dollars to buy the same basket of goods and services.

The cost of living varies from city to city and from state to state. In the United States, for example, Alaska has the highest cost of living; Arkansas has the lowest. The American Chamber of Commerce Researchers Association

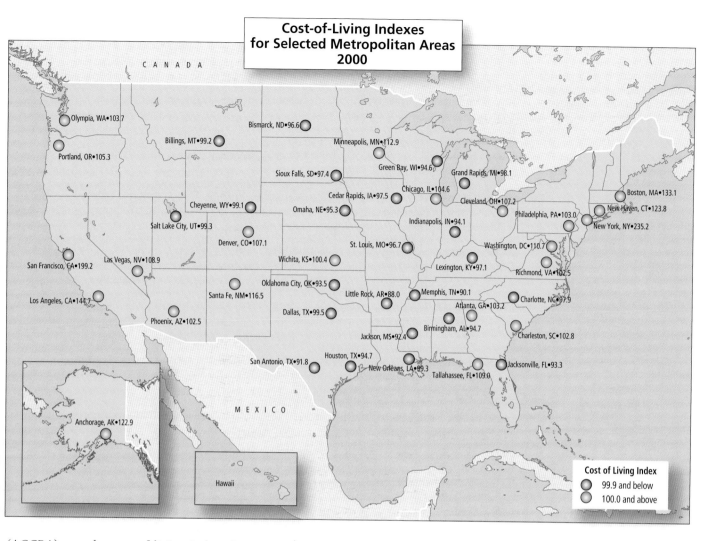

Cost-of-Living Indexes for Selected Metropolitan Areas 2000

Olympia, WA•103.7
Portland, OR•105.3
Billings, MT•99.2
Bismarck, ND•96.6
Minneapolis, MN•112.9
Green Bay, WI•94.6
Grand Rapids, MI•98.1
Boston, MA•133.1
New Haven, CT•123.8
Sioux Falls, SD•97.4
Cedar Rapids, IA•97.5
Chicago, IL•104.6
Cleveland, OH•107.2
Philadelphia, PA•103.0
New York, NY•235.2
Cheyenne, WY•99.1
Omaha, NE•95.3
Indianapolis, IN•94.1
Salt Lake City, UT•99.3
Denver, CO•107.1
St. Louis, MO•96.7
Washington, DC•110.7
San Francisco, CA•199.2
Las Vegas, NV•108.9
Wichita, KS•100.4
Lexington, KY•97.1
Richmond, VA•102.5
Oklahoma City, OK•93.5
Little Rock, AR•88.0
Memphis, TN•90.1
Charlotte, NC•97.9
Los Angeles, CA•144.7
Santa Fe, NM•116.5
Atlanta, GA•103.2
Phoenix, AZ•102.5
Dallas, TX•99.5
Birmingham, AL•94.7
Charleston, SC•102.8
Jackson, MS•92.4
San Antonio, TX•91.8
Houston, TX•94.7
New Orleans, LA•99.3
Tallahassee, FL•109.0
Jacksonville, FL•93.3
Anchorage, AK•122.9

CANADA

MEXICO

Hawaii

Cost of Living Index
○ 99.9 and below
○ 100.0 and above

(ACCRA) sets the cost-of-living index. For purposes of comparison, ACCRA sets the median state's, New Mexico, cost of living index to equal 100. Thus, the cost-of-living index in Alaska for the year 2000 was 125.7, or 25.7 percent higher than the cost of living in New Mexico. For Arkansas, the cost-of-living index for 2000 was 92.3. Thus to maintain the same standard of living, an accountant from Arkansas who wants to take an accounting job in Alaska must be prepared to negotiate a higher salary for the Alaska job; to maintain her standard of living (to acquire the same basket of goods), the accountant will have to negotiate a salary in Alaska that is nearly 40 percent higher than her current salary in Arkansas.

Cost of living varies widely around the world. Some countries with significantly lower costs of living than the United States include Colombia and Hungary; countries with significantly higher costs of living than the United States include Switzerland and Argentina. While many factors contribute to these higher (or lower) costs of living, the basic question is still the same: What is the relative price of the same basket of goods in one country compared with another?

The standard of living for a person or a nation depends upon that person's or nation's capacity to consume goods and services. That capacity is determined, to a large extent, by the average relative prices facing that person or nation. The higher the average relative prices, the less consumption possible—all other things, including income, being equal. As economic growth is dependent on consumption, economists need to measure trends in the cost of living to determine and analyze growth trends.

Further Reading

Mankiw, N. G. *Principles of Economics*. 2nd ed. Fort Worth, Tex.: Harcourt College Publishers, 2001.

—*Phillip J. VanFossen*

In addition to preparing cost-of-living indexes (COLIs) for states, the American Chamber of Commerce Researchers Association also reports COLIs for selected metropolitan areas.

Credit

In the simplest terms, credit is a promise to pay. Sometimes credit is extended based on collateral, which is a tangible asset like a car or a house. Other times, credit is extended based on earnings potential of a business or individual. In both cases, credit is extended on the basis of character—that is, how likely a borrower is to repay the loan.

When a lending institution extends credit, it creates both an asset and a liability on its balance sheet. The asset is the interest it hopes to receive on the amount lent. The liability is the amount of money given to the borrower. In an ideal world, borrowers would repay their loans in full, including the interest. In the real world, borrowers default, go bankrupt, and get behind in payments. Lending institutions must balance the risk of lending with the reward of profit.

Brief History of Twentieth-Century Banking

Originally, banks were independent operations. They could practice investment banking alongside commercial banking, and many did. Their primary lending business was commercial paper. Commercial paper is a short-term loan (usually 30–90 days) made to businesses. These loans are used to pay for items like an increase in seasonal inventory. Banks used other available funds for investing in bonds and the stock market. Banks were legally prohibited from making real estate loans because real estate loans were not considered liquid enough to sustain normal banking operations. Each bank issued its own money, and the money was only as good as the bank that issued it.

During the Civil War, the federal government stepped in and created a national currency (National Currency Act, 1863) and a national bank (National Bank Act, 1864). The purpose for creating these was to sel

An illustration from the Civil War era. Inside the U.S. Treasury, then located on Wall Street in New York City, people buy the first-ever U.S. bonds, which were issued by the government to raise money for the war.

In 1930 worried customers line up to withdraw their money from the Bowery Savings Bank in New York City.

bonds to finance the war. In effect, the nation's debt was tied to its currency—a relationship that still exists and influences inflation, interest rates, credit, and the amount of money in circulation.

Although the national currency could be cashed in (for gold) at any national bank or at the national Treasury, there was no federal guarantee of the solvency of those banks. Such guarantee would come in 1933, with the creation of the Federal Deposit Insurance Corporation (FDIC). Prior to 1933, if a bank made bad decisions on extending credit, the bank would have to close when it ran out of funds.

Before the creation of the FDIC, the Federal Reserve Act of 1913 had established a system of 12 federal banks that functioned as a central banking system. These banks were to hold the idle reserves of national and county banks as a backup for banks in crisis. These 12 banks were located across the nation so that all other banks were within one day's travel of a Federal Reserve bank. If customers wanted their cash from a bank that did not have enough cash on hand, that bank could take its commercial paper and cash it in within 24 hours.

During and after the Great Depression, the economy came to a standstill because consumers were afraid to spend money, borrow money, or to put money in banks. By 1933, business had recovered somewhat, but consumers were still reluctant. The FDIC was created in 1933 to boost consumer confidence and to get people borrowing and spending again. Even with the guarantee that the federal government would back up money in any member bank, people still held on to their money. Not until after World War II did consumer borrowing and spending rise enough to rejuvenate the economy.

Another early piece of legislation that shaped credit in the United States is the Banking Act of 1935. This act changed the financial structure of the country by centralizing power within the Federal Reserve Board in Washington, D.C.; until then, most of the banking powerhouses were located in downtown Manhattan. The move marked the evolution from private banking to public banking and moved the Federal Reserve (often called the Fed) from banking into a regulatory function. The Fed now controlled interest rates, cash reserves, and some aspects

Lines of consumer credit can be accessed via credit cards.

of investment banking. Meanwhile the Banking Act loosened the requirements for real estate lending, marking a move from short-term, liquid lending to longer-term lending on hard-to-move assets.

The post–World War II era brought another round of changes in the lending environment. By 1950, Diners' Club had come out with the first modern credit card. No-down-payment loans became popular, along with federally guaranteed home mortgages (amortized to make them profitable for the lending institution), and personal loans with easier terms. In the second half of the twentieth century, this relaxation of lending terms resulted in much higher debt burdens, both for the consumer and commercial interests. The economy benefited because mass production requires mass consumption. As consumers bought more homes, cars, and products, businesses had to expand, hire more people, and buy more supplies to keep up with the demand. Both businesses and consumers needed loans to manage those increases. The economy picked up and, even though it has experienced a few recessions, has continued to grow into the early twenty-first century. The availability of easy credit has fueled much of this growth.

The Gold Standard

The ready availability of credit is partly attributable to the switch from the gold standard to our current system. From 1879 to 1932, all U.S. money was tied to the gold standard. Gold backed the currency and could be bought at a set price: $20.67 per ounce. At any time, individuals could go to a bank and demand their money in gold. When the gold was taken out of the banks and ultimately the Treasury, interest rates rose, causing the country to go into a recession.

In 1932, the United States switched to a gold-exchange standard. Instead of the dollar being backed only by gold, it was now backed by both gold and commercial paper. Using commercial paper, or short-term loans, for collateral, implied that good loans were the same as "money in the bank," or in the Federal Reserve, to be exact. This expanded the amount of currency available in the United States, but the international markets still held to a semblance of the gold standard. A foreign government could still convert its dollars into gold from the Treasury. Gold was still leaving the country, decreasing the federal reserves.

In 1971 President Richard Nixon signed a bill that halted the conversion of dollars into gold, even for foreign countries. This, in effect, ended any ties to the original gold standard. From that point on, the dollar has been backed by the solvency of the U.S. government; the dollar is legal tender simply because the government says it is. Its value expands and contracts with the economy. This enables the Federal Reserve to control the amount of money in circulation by extending or restricting the extension of credit.

Commercial Lending

The U.S. economy is strong because of the nation's industrial supremacy. However, industrial supremacy depends on mass production, which depends on mass consumption, which depends on mass credit—to both businesses and the consumer. Supply (production) and demand (consumption) working together properly ead to more jobs, which may result in more potential borrowers.

The corporate tax structure of the United States heavily favors debt financing over equity capital. For example, interest paid on corporate debt is tax deductible but dividends paid out are not only taxed, but also taxed twice, first to the corporation and then to the shareholder who receives them. In other words, it pays to be in debt.

Debt can take many forms—commercial paper, construction loans, business loans, or bonds. Lending institutions must decide how much risk is involved in lending to a particular business. In the past, that risk was determined by past financial performance or a close examination of a company's finances, particularly for small businesses. Lenders have now turned to risk ratings of business owners. Personal credit history is a good indicator of how a small-business owner will pay the company's bills. Risk ratings compare personal credit history against other borrowers who fit the same profile. These profiles are created by companies that specialize in risk ratings. Lenders can purchase risk ratings on anyone with a personal credit history. Lending with this method gives the bank a better idea of the potential risk and eliminates the need for extensive study of a company's financial statements.

Companies can also become borrowers by issuing bonds. They sell bonds to investors at a specific interest rate. When the bonds mature, the company redeems the bonds at the stated rate. Bonds give companies the opportunity to raise capital without using a lending institution. The interest paid is determined by the current interest rate. The main issue for the company is convincing investors that the company is a good risk.

Consumerism, Credit, and the Economy
In one sense, consumer spending drives the economy. As evidenced by the economy's virtual standstill during the Great

---

Credit Time Line

1863–1864
National Currency Act and National Bank Act are passed to help finance the Civil War.

⬇

1913
The Federal Reserve Act creates a central banking system.

⬇

1929
The stock market crash signals the onset of the Great Depression.

⬇

1932
United States switches to a gold-exchange standard; the dollar is backed by both gold and commercial paper (short-term loans).

⬇

1933
In the wake of mass bank failures, the Federal Deposit Insurance Corporation (FDIC) is created.

⬇

1935
The Banking Act centralizes financial power within the Federal Reserve.

⬇

1950
Diners' Club issues the first modern credit card.

⬇

1971
Nixon administration terminates the gold standard.

Depression and for more than a decade after, consumer spending and borrowing depend on consumer confidence in the financial future. When fear sets in, people stop spending. When consumers stop spending, the economy slows and finally grinds to a halt. Banks actually see an increase in deposits as people begin saving for an uncertain future.

In the early twenty-first century, the amount of money Americans spend far outweighs the amount of money they take home in a paycheck or in investment income. The reason they can do so is credit. Credit comes in a variety of forms—mortgages, car loans, personal loans, student loans, and credit cards. Over time, lending institutions and the federal government have eased the requirements for extending credit by offering easy terms and requiring little or no down payment. The federal government's backing of loans gives confidence to both the borrower and the lender. Credit profiling permits easier identification of potential financial deadbeats. More credit has been and can be extended to more people.

The question arises: Why would so many people go into debt so easily? The short explanation is the American Dream—the dream of owning a home, nice cars and furnishings, and to have money for leisure activities. Many Americans have come to view this dream as their rightful heritage. More and more, that dream is within reach through credit.

The perceived upside of consumer credit is that it allows individuals to increase their social status through the accumulation of more and better goods. If consumer credit is managed well by using it for investment purposes, for example, purchasing a home, it can increase a person's net worth. Once the loan is repaid (provided the homeowner remains in possession long enough to see the home's price increase), the home becomes an asset with real value.

However, if consumer credit is used to purchase consumable goods, it actually decreases a person's net worth. Automobiles, which appear to be an asset, depreciate rapidly. As a car ages, it becomes a liability as repairs are more necessary and more frequent. The amount of interest paid on those kinds of loans increases the price of those goods tremendously and with little or nothing to show for it in the end.

Credit is a double-edged sword. On the one hand, easy availability entices consumers to borrow and spend, which increases demand, which turns the wheels of production and boosts the economy. This upward cycle points to prosperity all around. On the other hand, unwise use of credit can turn prosperity to poverty for some when individuals or businesses overextend themselves to the point of financial ruin. The wisest use of credit is to increase net worth while borrowing at the lowest interest rate possible.

Further Reading

Bazerman, Max H. *Smart Money Decisions.* New York: John Wiley & Sons, 1999.

Grant, James. *Money of the Mind: Borrowing and Lending in America from the Civil War to Michael Milken.* New York: Farrar Straus & Giroux, 1992.

Leach, William. *Land of Desire: Merchants, Power, and the Rise of a New American Culture.* New York: Pantheon Books, 1993.

Schor, Juliet B. *The Overspent American: Upscaling, Downshifting, and the New Consumer.* New York: Basic Books, 1998.

Twitchell, James B. *Lead Us into Temptation: The Triumph of American Materialism.* New York: Columbia University Press, 1999.

—Stephanie Buckwalter

Credit Cards and Debit Cards

Credit cards are used in millions of transactions each year. Consumers use credit cards to buy all kinds of goods, to buy food, and for large purchases like appliances and travel. Businesses also rely on credit card transactions for purchases and sales. A whole industry has developed focused on credit cards, debit cards, and electronic transfers of funds. Companies in this industry offer, manage, and manufacture the products and services used in the credit card industry.

What is a credit card? It is a small plastic card containing a means of personal identification and account information. The card authorizes the person named on it to charge purchases using his or her account. Each month, the holder of the card receives a bill based on those charges. Most credit cards are issued by banks, retail stores, or gas companies. Visa and MasterCard are the largest of the bank-card companies. Sears offers the Discover Card. Not-for-profit organizations and even professional baseball and football teams have begun to issue credit cards.

Plastic Money?: The Nature of Credit Cards

Some people refer to credit cards as plastic money. When they do, however, they are making a mistake. Credit cards are not money. One characteristic of money is that money is a medium of exchange. By itself, a credit card is not a payment for a good or service; it is a promise to pay. A credit card transaction is most often a loan made by the card issuer to the cardholder. Like other loans, credit card loans must be repaid. After a grace period (often 25 days) during which interest is not charged, consumers pay interest on the balance they owe until it is paid off.

It is common today for young people as well as adults to use credit cards. Many teenagers about to enter college receive unsolicited credit cards in the mail. Parents often want young people to learn about credit cards, but they also worry about the potential for abuse. Secured credit cards are popular with people who are new to using credit cards and with those who have a bad credit history. A secured credit loan involves making a deposit to a bank or other financial institution. The credit limit of the credit card may equal the amount deposited.

Credit limits are among the several factors to consider when obtaining and using a credit card. A higher credit limit gives the cardholder increased flexibility but can also lead to high balances owed, which can be difficult to pay off. Other considerations include the interest rates charged on the unpaid balance and other fees imposed by the credit card issuer.

Interest rates can vary from card issuer to card issuer by several percentage points. Some credit card companies offer a low annual percentage rate (APR) of interest for the first few months of card use and then increase the rate. Card users likely to keep a high balance on their accounts should consider shopping for a low APR.

However, interest rates may be related to fees. Obtaining a low interest rate might require payment of a high annual fee to the card issuer. Card users who pay their balance in full every month might benefit from using a higher-interest card if it comes with a low annual fee or no fee. Other fees may include charges for late or missed payments, charges for exceeding credit limits, and charges made for cash withdrawals.

See also:
Compound Interest; Credit;
Credit History; Money.

Choosing a Credit Card

Credit cards differ in kinds of services. Variations to consider when choosing a card include:
1. Interest rates on purchases and cash advances;
2. Whether an annual membership fee is required;
3. The number of merchants who accept the card;
4. Length of grace period before interest is charged;
5. Rewards for the cardholder including cash-back payments, gifts, frequent flyer miles, or discounts on certain purchases;
6. Travel services like covering the insurance deductible on rental cars, discounts on hotels, travel life insurance, or check cashing privileges.

Protection and Regulation

Credit cards contain valuable information, including the cardholder's name, account number, and the card's expiration date. This information can be misused if it falls into the wrong hands. Some people discover after loss or theft of a credit card that it has been used within hours to purchase thousands of dollars worth of goods. Cardholders are advised, accordingly, to use their cards carefully—never giving account information to a telephone solicitor or to people or organizations (online or in person) with whom they are not familiar—and to report lost or stolen cards promptly.

To further protect consumers, credit card loans are regulated by state and federal laws. The Equal Credit Opportunity Act, for example, was passed to ensure that all consumers have an equal chance to receive credit. The Equal Credit Opportunity Act makes it illegal to discriminate against credit applicants on the basis of sex, marital status, race, national origin, religion, age, or because they receive public assistance.

The Truth-in-Lending Act requires that creditors disclose the cost of credit in simple terms. The lender must state the percentage costs of borrowing in terms of the annual percentage rate (APR). The Truth-in-Lending Act also protects against unauthorized use of credit cards. If your card is lost or stolen, you are liable for not more than $50 of unauthorized charges, provided you report the lost or stolen card promptly. After notification, you cannot be held responsible for any unauthorized charges.

History of the Credit Card Industry

During the 1920s some individual firms, oil companies and hotels among them, began issuing credit cards to customers for direct purchases of goods and services. These early credit cards simply extended the revolving charge accounts many businesses had offered to customers. Use of credit cards increased greatly after World War II as more Americans began to travel. Credit cards were a convenience to consumers who purchased goods and services from large national hotel chains and oil companies.

The next step was to introduce universal credit cards; a universal card was one that could be used with different, unrelated businesses. The first credit cards were actually charge cards. Charge cards require the holder to pay off the balance in full each billing cycle. The cardholder paid an annual fee to use the card, but did not pay interest if the bill was paid on time. In 1950 the Diners' Club issued a charge card that could be used in different restaurants, not merely those owned by one company. The American Express Company soon followed, establishing a major universal charge card in 1958. American Express contracted with businesses whereby participating merchants agreed to pay a service charge to American Express for credit card transactions. In turn, participating merchants hoped that the convenience of using the card would attract additional customers to their businesses.

The credit card industry changed dramatically when banks entered the picture. People in the banking industry took note of the success of American Express and other credit card firms. Bankers recognized that credit cards could become the

The Equal Credit Opportunity Act

The Equal Credit Opportunity Act was passed in 1974 to abolish discriminatory practices in consumer lending. For example, in deciding whether to extend credit to an individual, a company may not:

- Consider gender, race, marital status, national origin, or religion;
- Consider the race of the people in the neighborhood where the applicant wishes to buy, refinance, or improve a house with borrowed money;
- Consider age, unless
  (a) the applicant is under 18
  (b) the applicant is over 62 and the creditor will favor the applicant because of age
  (c) it is used as part of a valid scoring system to determine overall credit (for example, if an applicant is close to retirement age, his income might be expected to drop);
- Refuse to consider public assistance income the same way as other income;
- Discount income because of sex or marital status. For example, a creditor cannot count a man's salary at 100 percent and a woman's at 75 percent. A creditor may not assume a woman of childbearing age will stop working to raise children;
- Discount or refuse to consider income because it comes from part-time employment or pension, annuity, or retirement benefit programs;
- Refuse to consider regular alimony, child support, or separate maintenance payments.

basis for making highly convenient and widespread loans to consumers. Banks began issuing credit cards and soon formed associations to act as clearinghouses for transactions and to promote their own card brands. Banks are now consolidated into two major associations of card issuers, Visa and MasterCard.

The process of credit card transactions has changed greatly since the 1950s and 1960s. Originally a small metal plate similar to the license you might find on the collar of a dog was embossed with the name, address, and account number of the customer. Businesses purchased machines that would imprint the customer information onto charge slips. This technology has been replaced for the most part by the magnetic stripe on credit cards. Cards with magnetic stripes permitted merchants and eventually cardholders to register a transaction simply by swiping a credit card

The Truth-in-Lending Act

Originally enacted in July 1969 as part of the Consumer Protection Act, the Truth-in-Lending Act (TILA) requires that lenders clearly and accurately disclose the terms of the credit they extend. The law also provides consumers with a chance to back out of certain loans within a certain time frame.

The most important aspect of TILA for consumers is probably Regulation Z, which covers credit cards, personal loans, home mortgages, and other forms of consumer debt. Under Regulation Z, lenders must disclose the following information:

- Finance Charge, or the amount charged to the consumer for the credit;
- Amount Financed, or the amount that is being borrowed;
- Total of Payments, or the total amount of the periodic payments required;
- Total Sales Price, or the total cost of the purchase on credit, including the down payment and periodic payments;
- Annual Percentage Rate (APR), or the cost of the credit on a yearly basis.

The APR is important because it enables consumers to easily compare one credit offer with another. Companies that do not comply with the TILA can be sued by consumers. If a TILA violation is proven in court, sizable fines can be imposed.

through an electronic recording-and-transfer device. The magnetic stripe contains the account number of the cardholder. It allows merchants to enter and verify

Actress Anna Maria Alberghetti points to oversized Diners' Club card being held by Jules Podell, the director of the Copacabana nightclub (left), and Diners' Club chairman Ralph Schneider.

Credit Cards and Debit Cards   321

Boys buying sports gear with a credit card.

account numbers rapidly and accurately. Magnetic stripes offer three key advantages: They reduce transaction costs by reducing paperwork; they increase the number of transactions that can be handled; and they reduce the danger of credit card fraud.

The expansion of electronic transfers of funds has continued to bring changes and growth to the credit card industry. A major change came with the introduction and proliferation of automated teller machines (ATMs). ATMs had originally been a convenient service for people living in urban areas. When systems were developed to provide automated teller services in remote locations, people in small towns, rural areas, and travelers abroad gained access to ATM services.

Since 1989 the number of Americans with at least one credit card has increased steadily.

General Purpose Credit Cards 1989 to 1998

| Year | Percent of families with general purpose credit card | Median number of cards | Median balance | Percent who: | | |
				Almost always pay off the balance	Sometimes pay off the balance	Hardly ever pay off the balance
1989	56.0	2	$1,300	52.9	21.2	25.8
1992	62.4	2	$1,100	53.0	19.6	27.4
1995	66.4	2	$1,600	52.4	20.1	27.5
1998	67.5	2	$1,900	53.8	19.3	26.9

Note: General purpose credit cards include MasterCard, Visa, Optima, and Discover cards. Excludes cards used only for business purposes. All dollar figures are in constant 1998 dollars.
Source: Board of Governors of the Federal Reserve System.

Debit Cards

As more and more merchants came to accept credit cards and ATMs became more widely available, the stage was set for the emergence of the debit card, a recent arrival on the plastic card scene. A bank issues a debit card to provide consumers with electronic access to the funds in their accounts. The procedure for using a debit card closely resembles the procedure for using a credit card. In each case, consumers hand the card to the cashier or swipe it themselves through the card-reading device.

Two important differences exist between credit cards and debit cards. First, a debit card allows a consumer to pay for a purchase through an immediate deduction from his or her checking account. Using the debit card is thus very similar to writing a check. In fact, debit cards are rapidly replacing checks as a method of payment. Debit cards are generally more convenient because they are more widely accepted than personal checks. Debit cards can also be used to withdraw cash from ATMs.

The second difference is that, unlike credit cards, debit cards do not provide consumers with the advantage of a "float" on their money. Float refers to the period between the time when a check is written and the time when it is cashed (the money would earn interest in that interval). Credit-card holders receive float for the 25 days they are not charged interest on purchases. As payment for the debit card transaction is withdrawn immediately from a checking account, there is no float in a debit card transaction.

Are debit cards plastic money? When consumers use debit cards for purchases, they are basically instructing the banks involved to transfer money directly from their checking accounts to the stores' bank accounts. Use of a debit card does not create a loan, as is usually the case in a credit card transaction; in effect, debit card account money is checking account money. In this respect, debit cards really are plastic money.

The credit card and debit card industry will almost certainly continue to expand

and change. International use is widespread. E-commerce on the Internet has opened new opportunities for online merchants to accept credit cards and new challenges for banks and processors to provide secure and compliant transaction services.

A woman pays for groceries with a debit card; she inputs her personal identification number (PIN) on the keypad, just as she would if she were taking money out of an ATM.

Further Reading

Lee, Dwight R., and Richard B. McKenzie. *Getting Rich in America.* New York: HarperBusiness, 1999.

Morton, John S., and Mark C. Schug. *Financial Fitness for Life: Bringing Home the Gold.* New York: National Council on Economic Education, 2001.

Ryan, Joan S. *Managing Your Finances.* Cincinnati, Ohio: South-Western Educational Publishing, 1997.

—*Mark C. Schug*

Credit History

Anyone who has filled out a credit application has a credit history. The information on credit applications is sent to a credit reporting agency (CRA) to verify the information submitted and to acquire any additional information about a requestor's ability to take on debt. If no information currently exists on that requestor, a credit file is created for future use, even if the credit application is not approved.

The credit file serves two purposes. First, it gives basic information about the requestor, salary and address, for instance. The next time a credit application comes through, it will be checked to see if any information has changed. If so, the CRA tracks those changes. The second purpose benefits only the CRA. CRAs sell information to third parties from their databases. Legally they are not allowed to sell credit payment information, but the basic "header" information is fair game. Header information typically includes full name, birth date, current and previous employer, position, current and two previous addresses, marital status, and spouse's name.

This information can be sold to anyone who wants to pay for it, including direct marketing firms, information brokers who resell it to others, lawyers, or private detectives.

In addition to the header, a credit file contains payment history information. Most of the payment information is from lenders who are paid monthly, for example, credit and charge card issuers and lending institutions that hold mortgages or any other kind of loan. The information provided by the lender includes how long the borrower takes to make a payment—30, 60, 90, or 120 days. When the borrower is involved in a bankruptcy or dispute, that becomes part of the credit file, too. Other kinds of businesses may file a report with the CRA for a borrower who is seriously delinquent in paying or when the account is turned over to a collection agency. These include local merchants, landlords, utility companies, medical and other professional service providers, and child support delinquencies in excess of $1,000.

Two more items go into a credit file: the names of creditors and others who have requested a copy of your information and public record information. Although public records are just that—information that is available to anyone—CRAs pay other companies to collect that information to include in credit files. The public records searched relate to a potential borrower's ability to repay loans. Public records include liens, bankruptcies, foreclosures, criminal records, divorce, and legal judgments.

The Importance of Credit History

What does all this information mean and who looks at it? The primary audience for a credit history report is lenders. Lenders want to know how safe it is to lend money. Bad loans mean lost revenue. Although a borrower does not have to have a perfect credit history to get a loan or receive credit, the lender has to balance the good credit risks against the bad ones. The bad credit risks will have a harder time getting credit, but will not be shut out entirely.

Increasingly, employers and insurance companies are requesting, and being granted,

---

Fair Credit Reporting Act

Key Provisions

- People can find out what is in their files
- People must be told if information in their files has been used against them
- People can dispute inaccurate information
- Inaccurate information must be corrected or deleted
- Outdated information may not be reported
- Access to files is limited
- Consent is required for reports that are provided to employers or reports that contain medical information
- People may choose to have their information excluded from CRA lists for unsolicited credit and insurance offers
- People may seek damages from violators

Credit cards should be used prudently, since a bad credit report can cause problems in the future.

access to credit files. Employers use the information to judge personal integrity and the risk of illegal activity from desperate debtors. Insurance companies use the credit histories to check for information on any major medical problems.

Consumers have three major national credit bureaus: Equifax, Trans Union Corporation, and Experian (formerly TRW). Almost all local credit bureaus are members of or are affiliated with one of these three.

Lenders and other parties can request a report from one or all three credit bureaus. Each bureau collects information independently of the others. Their reports differ in format, but all contain the same kind of information. However, each may collect different pieces of information. For example, a bankruptcy report may include a long list of debts. The credit bureau may not record all of them, and the three credit bureaus may not record the same debts.

In 1968 Congress passed the Consumer Credit Protection Act to protect individuals with a credit history. The specific subchapter of the act related to credit history is the Fair Credit Reporting Act. The two major tenets of the act are that credit reports must

Credit Report Problems

Possible Problems with Credit Reports

- Inaccurate credit information
- Out-of-date credit information
- Incorrect personal information, such as name, address, marital status, birth date
- Crossed information from consumers with similar names
- Information left on report that should have been removed
- Identity theft

be accurate and that the CRA must protect the privacy of the consumer. Consumers are allowed to request a copy of their own credit report and should do so yearly.

Most credit history problems relate to inaccurate or out-of-date information. When this occurs, consumers can clean up their credit reports by contacting the CRA directly and asking for a review of items under question. Credit repair organizations offer to do the same for a fee. However, these organizations are bound by the same laws as the consumer. To ensure compliance, the Credit Repair Organizations Act lays out the requirements for the practice of credit cleaning plus the relationship between the consumer and the repair organization. The repair organization must provide a written contract that clearly states the services offered and also states that the repair organization will not try to remove any accurate information from the consumer's credit history, even if it is negative. The contract must also contain a "buyer's remorse" clause that gives the consumer 72 hours to cancel the contract without penalty.

Some of the more common problems not related to actual bad credit are wrong header information, crossed information from consumers with similar names, and information left on the report that should have been removed. Bankruptcy information remains on a credit report for 10 years, most other information for seven years. Some information stays longer because of state statutes. Other entries—criminal records and lawsuits—may remain indefinitely.

One problem with the relatively free flow of information is identity theft. Consumers should regularly review their files to clean them up and to check for unauthorized use of their names or credit. Identity theft occurs when someone collects personal data like that found in the header of a credit file and uses it to assume that person's identity or to request that additional credit cards be sent to a new address. The credit card industry has no standards or regulations to stop identity theft; thus it is important that consumers check their credit reports regularly.

Business Credit History

Businesses develop a credit history in much the same way as do individuals, especially small businesses that establish a credit history by acquiring a credit card in the name of the business or corporation. All the same rules apply. In addition to the credit bureaus tracing business credit cards, business credit is tracked by CRAs like D&B (formerly Dun & Bradstreet).

D&B is the largest of the business reporting agencies, with information on 70 million companies worldwide. It tracks credit history including payment habits, collections, and public information. It also tracks sales, assets, liabilities, and profits. D&B then produces reports based on its data to help other businesses, lenders, and investors make decisions based on the total financial picture of a business. This allows others to gauge their risk in dealing with or investing in a company.

In both the personal and business credit reporting industry, a trend toward creating what is commonly called credit scoring, risk scoring, or a risk rating is evident. This process produces a single number, or score, that predicts the borrower's payment habits. The higher the number, the lower the risk involved in extending credit. The score is obtained by comparing a large sample of borrowers and identifying the profiles of low-risk borrowers. No one-size-fits-all

Credit Report

YOUR CREDIT REPORT
As of October 10, 2003

Personal Information
Jane Doe
555 Main Street
Small Town, CA 99999

Social Security Number: 555-55-555

Date of Birth: January 1, 1980

A credit report contains not only current information about where the subject lives but also previous addresses going back several years.

Previous Address(es)
2 South Road
Small Town, CA 99999

Some credit reports (not all) give employment history.

Employment History
CyberWidgets
Silicon Valley, CA 99999

Employment Date: May 2000

Widgets Online
Silicon Valley, CA 99999

Employment Date: September 2002

A credit report includes publicly available information collected from federal, state, and local courts. This may include bankruptcies, court judgments, foreclosures, and even marriages.

Public Records
No bankruptcies on file
No liens on file
No foreclosures on file
No judgments on file
No marital status on file

If a debt is not repaid and the debtor turns the account over to a collection agency, this is noted in the credit history.

Collections Accounts
No collections on file

Credit Information

There are several different kinds of accounts: a credit card is a revolving account; a college loan is an installment account.

Company Name	Account Number	Date Opened	Last Activity	Type of Account and Status	Credit Limit	Balance	Amount Past Due
American Express	99999999999999	04/1999	09/2003	Revolving PAYS AS AGREED	$6,000	$2,466	0

Prior Paying History
30 days past due 04 times; 60 days past due 02 times; 90 + days past due 00 times

This section notes the number of times the debtor has been late with payments.

Company Name	Account Number	Date Opened	Last Activity	Type of Account and Status	Credit Limit	Balance	Amount Past Due
MasterCard	55555555555555	01/2002	05/2003	Revolving PAYS AS AGREED	$2,000	$1,100	0

Prior Paying History
30 days past due 01 time(s); 60 days past due 00 time(s); 90 + days past due 00 time(s)

Company Name	Account Number	Date Opened	Last Activity	Type of Account and Status	Credit Limit	Balance	Amount Past Due
Auto Finance International	G204576KR	11/1999	1/2001	Installment REPOSESSION	$13,500	$6,755	$300

Prior Paying History
30 days past due 09 time(s); 60 days past due 06 time(s); 90 + days past due 03 time(s)
AUTO REPOSSESSED

Loans that are not repaid are reported on the credit report, even, as in this case, when the car has already been repossessed.

Company Name	Account Number	Date Opened	Last Activity	Type of Account and Status	Credit Limit	Balance	Amount Past Due
California Student Loan Corporation	222222222222 INDIVIDUAL ACCOUNT	10/1998	02/1999	Installment PAYS AS AGREED	$3,800	$0	

Prior Paying History
Paid Account. Zero balance

Repaid loans and closed credit cards remain on the credit report.

Additional Information

Companies that Requested Your File
October 10, 2003   Check YR Credit Corporation
April 23, 2003   Friendly Cell Phone Co.
November 13, 2002   Home Furnishings Warehouse
January 4, 2001   MasterCard Co.

Consumers have the right to know who has been checking up on them. Credit reports list requests for credit history information, which might occur when someone sets up a new cell phone account, requests a line of credit from a store, or gets a new credit card.

Identity Theft

Although the Internet has done much to make consumers' lives easier, it has also made the lives of thieves easier. Identity theft, wherein a thief gains access to someone's personal information (Social Security number, credit card account numbers, and so on) and runs up charges on the innocent person's accounts, is on the rise.

The Federal Trade Commission (FTC) recommends taking the following steps to limit the chances of identity theft.

- Order a credit report from each of the three major credit bureaus once a year. One of the most common ways that consumers find out that they have been victims of identity theft is when they try to make a major purchase, like a house or a car. The deal can be lost or delayed while the credit report mess is straightened out. Knowing what is in a credit report allows time to fix problems before they jeopardize a major financial transaction.
- Place passwords on credit card, bank, and phone accounts. Avoid using easily available information like birth date, mother's maiden name, or a series of consecutive numbers. Many businesses still have a line on their applications for mother's maiden name; use a password instead.
- Ask about information security procedures in the workplace. Find out who has access to personal information and verify that records are kept in a secure location. Ask about the disposal procedures for those records.
- Secure personal information at home, especially if you have roommates, employ outside help, or are having service work done in your home.
- Do not give out personal information on the phone, through the mail, or over the Internet unless you initiated the contact. Identity thieves may pose as representatives of banks, Internet service providers, and even government employees. Before sharing any personal information, confirm that you are dealing with a legitimate organization.
- Deposit outgoing mail in post office collection boxes or at your local post office rather than in an unsecured mailbox. At home, promptly remove mail from the mailbox.
- To thwart an identity thief who may pick through trash or recycling bins to capture personal information, tear or shred charge receipts, copies of credit applications, insurance forms, physician statements, checks and bank statements, expired charge cards, and credit offers received in the mail.
- Before revealing any personally identifying information (for example, on an application), find out how it will be used and secured, and whether it will be shared with others. Ask if there is a choice about the use of the information. Can one choose to have it kept confidential?
- Do not carry a Social Security card; keep it in a secure place.
- Give out Social Security number only when absolutely necessary. Ask to use other kinds of identifiers when possible.
- Carry only the identification information and the number of credit and debit cards that are actually needed.
- Pay attention to billing cycles. Follow up with creditors if bills do not arrive on time. A missing credit card bill could mean an identity thief has changed the billing address.
- Be wary of promotional scams. Identity thieves may use phony offers to get personal information.
- Keep purses or wallets in a safe place at work.

Of course, not every instance of identity theft can be prevented. The FTC recommends that all consumers order copies of their credit reports at least once a year to verify that no one else is incurring debts in their name. Any false information should be immediately reported to the credit report issuer so that it can be investigated and corrected. The FTC maintains a Web site for more information about identity theft (http://www.consumer.gov/idtheft/index.html).

model for extending credit exists. Models vary depending on the kind of loan and the collateral. Some companies specialize in creating these models and selling the results. Large financial institutions may develop their own statistical models.

Risk rating does not replace credit history. Rather, the risk rating is based on the analysis of a large sample of credit files. The risk rating is not actually part of the credit file available to the consumer. The CRA owns the rating and is not legally required to disclose it to the borrower. A risk rating cannot be used as a reason for refusing credit. Refusal must be tied to specific items in the credit file.

Consumer credit bureaus have used risk ratings for years, but the business credit industry has begun their use relatively recently. This development is particularly important for small businesses. With credit scoring, the labor-intensive analysis and tracking of business plans and financials are reduced. Statistical models allow lenders to use objective data to predict payment habits. Low-risk business applicants can be pre-approved with no personal interaction up front and little monitoring.

With credit history, time is on the borrower's side. Most negative information eventually rolls off the report, usually in seven to 10 years. In the meantime, individuals and businesses should review their credit reports annually as part of managing their finances, correct any errors promptly, and work to guard against identity theft.

Further Reading

Caouette, John B., Edward I. Altman, and Paul Narayanan. *Managing Credit Risk: The Next Great Financial Challenge.* New York: John Wiley & Sons, 1998.

Federal Trade Commission. *Building a Better Credit Record.* Washington, D.C.: Federal Trade Commission, 1997.

Jasper, Margaret C. *Credit Cards and the Law.* 2nd ed. Dobbs Ferry, N.Y.: Oceana Publications, 2000.

Leonard, Robin. *Credit Repair.* 4th ed. Berkeley, Calif.: Nolo, 2000.

—Stephanie Buckwalter

Cultural Difference

Culture influences consumer and business attitudes, decision making, and behaviors. Cultures are distinguished from one another in many areas, including value systems, legends and beliefs, religions, daily habits and routines, legal systems, ceremonies and celebrations, etiquette, and material goods. Fashions may change from decade to decade, or even year to year, but culture typically evolves and changes through generations. Cultural heritage has a profound influence on how and what people buy as well as how businesses operate. Cultures vary from one region of the world to another, from one country to another, and even among subgroups within one country.

When interacting with other cultures, businesspeople should consider a number of factors.

1. What is the value of personal relationships to business success? If personal connections are crucial, how can someone from outside the culture best achieve those relationships?

2. How task- or deal-oriented is the culture? In other words, are conversations direct, frank, and efficient, with the expectation that progress will be fast? Or are communications indirect or infused with unstated requests and assumptions?

3. Does the culture place importance on authority and hierarchy, or is it more egalitarian and informal, with cross-status communications being common?

4. How does the culture view time, punctuality, and the relative importance of short- versus long-term goals?

5. Does the preferred communication style require a reserved and quiet manner or is a more effusive and forceful manner expected?

6. What rules of etiquette are most important?

Answering these kinds of questions along with learning the core values of cultures can lead to fewer misunderstandings and more satisfying results in communications and negotiations.

International Cultural Differences

Some core values in the United States are individualism, equality, competition, and youth.

See also:
Globalization; International Trade; Market Research.

Japanese businessmen bow to each other in greeting rather than shake hands as is customary in many Western countries.

Some Asian cultures, however, value putting society above self, emphasizing the group and teamwork, and revering elders and authority figures. These differences may play out through business behaviors like giving awards. In the United States, managers often give recognition for employees' success. Contests among individual salespeople to win trips, merchandise, or bonuses are common. In Japan, however, recognition would be likely to go to entire teams or groups; bringing attention to oneself is discouraged. In U.S. advertising, an individual could be portrayed as winning a contest and boasting loudly about that success. In Japan, such behavior would be considered in poor taste.

Businesspeople in the United States typically value efficiency and punctuality; some Latin American countries, however, place less importance on timeliness but highly value relationship-building prior to conducting business. Meetings regularly begin late and last for extended periods, and business deals may take much longer to complete than in the United States. When members of various cultures meet to do business, misunderstandings can easily occur unless all are aware of and sensitive to the values, norms, and behaviors of other cultures.

Businesses study cultural differences using several methods. One approach is content analysis. Researchers catalog the content of large quantities of print or visual materials. They study advertisements in television or magazines, noting differences among cultures in the characteristics of models (e.g., age, gender, ethnic group), locations of settings, kinds of persuasive appeals, and frequency of advertised product categories. To discover interests and attitudes, researchers conduct content analyses of news media, researching the frequency of topics in articles and reports,

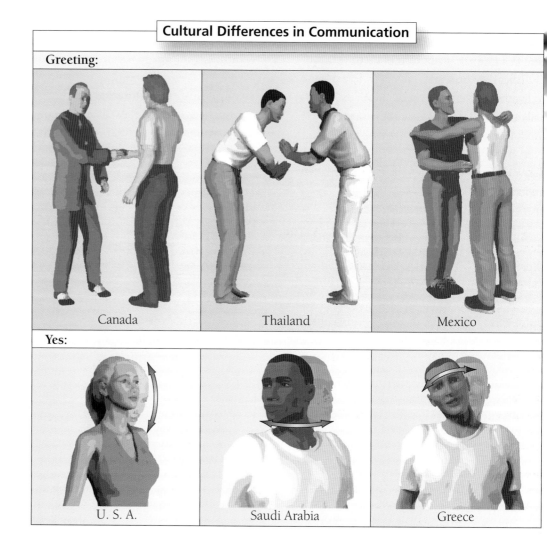

Cultural Differences in Communication

Greeting:

Canada   Thailand   Mexico

Yes:

U. S. A.   Saudi Arabia   Greece

The first McDonald's in New Delhi, India, opened in 1996. It was the first all-vegetarian McDonald's.

clothing worn by broadcasters, or the popularity of political or religious opinions.

Participant observation is a more personal approach to learning about a culture. A company might send a manager to live in another country and to record observations of the culture in a journal. A business producing breakfast cereal, for example, might send a manager to live in France to see what the French typically eat for breakfast, how they prepare their food, where they eat it, where they buy it, and even if most people actually eat breakfast. A faster, and perhaps more reliable, way to learn about another culture is to hire a local manager to explain or interpret the culture.

Differences in material goods are evident across cultures. Business gift–giving illustrates the material diversity among nations. Giving liquor to people from countries that are largely Islamic would be an unfortunate choice, as drinking alcohol runs counter to their religious beliefs. In China, business travelers should avoid giving clocks as gifts because they are a reminder of mortality. Although flowers are appropriate hostess gifts in many countries, the kind and number of flowers can give a message. In Europe, chrysanthemums are a funeral flower, and red roses are typically reserved for lovers. Giving 13 flowers would be a portent of bad luck. The quality of the wrapping of a gift will be very important in Japan,

as will giving a gift with a designer brand name. Also in Japan, businesspeople should avoid giving four of anything, another example of a number with negative connotations. In almost all cultures, however, thoughtful gifts for children are appreciated.

Choosing culturally appropriate gifts comes under the broader concept of expanding the distribution of a company's products beyond its national borders. Products have meanings beyond their utilitarian value. Some regions of the world will have cultures that are more accepting of a product than others. Trying to expand the distribution of a brand of liquor to Arab countries would be difficult, while European citizens would be more accepting. Sometimes producers make product modifications to suit individual cultures; for example, McDonald's restaurants offer teriyaki burgers in Japan or meatless sandwiches in India, where a Big Mac is known as a Maharaja Mac.

Subcultures within Nations

Many cultural groups, usually referred to as subcultures, exist within individual countries. Subcultures involve themselves in the larger national culture, but they may still identify with a smaller group. Subcultures exist based on geographic regions, on ethnicity or ancestral heritage, on demographics, on religion, or a variety of other characteristics.

Just as with national cultures, these subcultures share values and attitudes, behaviors, routines, or material goods that differ from other subgroups within the country.

Examples of these differences are easy to find. People living in the midwestern United States differ from those living in New England, who differ from those living in Texas. Some of the foods they eat are specific to their region. Their accents are often identifiable, and their leisure time activities may be concentrated outdoors or indoors, depending on the climate. Another example of subcultures would be those based on age. Age groups vary in behaviors. Teenagers differ from "baby-boomers," who differ from senior citizens in the kinds of clothes they wear, the music they choose, and the movies and television programs they typically watch. Religious groups are another example. Jews and Christians observe different holidays and days of worship, sing different religious songs, and read different religious books.

Numerous ethnic subcultures exist within the United States, with the three largest minority ethnic groups being African Americans, Hispanics, and Asian Americans. The term *Hispanic* refers to people who come from many areas: Mexico, Puerto Rico, Central America, and South America. Their preferences, values and attitudes may be unique to their culture although they may share a common language (with variations in dialect). Asian Americans show great diversity. They may have emigrated from many different nations: Japan, South or North Korea, China, or the Philippines. Their languages and foods are different, and their religious affiliations include Muslim, Buddhist, Christian, and Shinto. Their national histories have helped to shape their current behaviors.

The United States is not alone in this multiplicity of subcultures. For example, Indonesia has more than 300 ethnic subcultures, each with its own language, habits, traditions, and social norms. Businesses need to be aware of the differences among subgroups and to provide products that satisfy the unique needs of these groups as well as to communicate with them using effective words and images.

Cultures are learned, and they evolve through generations. Systems of values and beliefs, shaped by history, are the basis for cultures. The manifestation of cultures can be through languages, religions, legends, social rules, habits, and material goods like books, music, food, furniture, or clothing. The influence of culture is deep and strong. For a business to be successful in an international setting or even in a domestic setting with various subcultures, the company must research the culture and then apply the principles learned in a sensitive manner. The common phrase, "The world is getting smaller every day," is surely true from a communications standpoint, but it ignores the fact that people and cultures often celebrate and enjoy their differences and want to maintain their unique histories.

Infant Formula Controversy

In the 1970s and 1980s, Nestlé, a company that once controlled 50 percent of the world infant formula market, became the target of an international boycott in protest of its marketing of formula in developing nations. The controversy resulted from differences in needs and uses of the infant formula across cultures.

All parties agreed that breast milk was preferable to formula for infants up to one year old, but not all mothers were able to breastfeed their babies; in developed countries, formula was an appropriate alternative or supplement. In less developed countries, however, infant deaths sometimes resulted from mothers mixing formula with contaminated water or diluting it to make it last longer.

Nestlé eventually responded to the international pressure in a number of ways. They discouraged retailers from using special promotions for the formula. They stopped giving free formula samples to mothers except when those mothers were unable to breastfeed. They also stopped all advertising of infant formula. Marketing practices entirely appropriate in some nations created problems in others.

The debate concerning the use of infant formula has arisen again in sub-Saharan Africa, where AIDS is rampant. Numerous studies show that breastfeeding greatly increases the risk of transmission of AIDS from an infected mother to her infant. The current question is whether the risk of malnutrition from diluting the formula, or diarrhea from using contaminated water, is greater or less than the risk of AIDS transmission through breast milk.

Further Reading

Axtell, Roger, ed. *Do's and Taboos around the World.* 3rd ed. New York: Wiley, 1993.

Brake, Terence, Danielle Medina Walker, and Thomas Walker. *Doing Business Internationally: The Guide to Cross-cultural Success.* Burr Ridge, Ill.: Irwin Professional Pub., 1995.

Gesteland, Richard. *Cross-Cultural Business Behavior.* 2nd ed. Copenhagen: Copenhagen Business School Press, 1999.

—*Lois Smith*

Customer Service

Customer service is the process of giving customers what they want. In the service industries, customer service is most often defined by courteous, well-informed, well-trained employees. In retail, customer service can encompass everything from the customer-friendly layout of a store to generous return policies. In the online world, customer service can come in the form of easily navigable Web sites, quick "checkout," and reliable shipping. When competition is high and with customers increasingly knowledgeable about products and services, customer service is one of the key ways for businesses to differentiate themselves from one another.

The concept of customer service has its roots in the late nineteenth and early twentieth centuries, when department stores like Marshall Field's in Chicago and Macy's in New York City embraced new approaches to attracting and keeping customers. Depart-ment store owners built huge, inviting stores that included not only many kinds of consumer goods but also restaurants and elevators to facilitate shopping. Department store managers trained their clerks—mostly working-class, single women—to interact with customers, who were mainly upper-middle-class and upper-class women. The stores also offered home delivery and generous exchange policies to gain customers' loyalty.

Although customer service concepts and practices began to spread through different

See also:
E-Business; FedEx;
Retail and Wholesale.

An airline employee assists a customer with his ticket; face-to-face "service with a smile" is the most traditional kind of customer service.

Much contemporary customer service takes place on the telephone.

shown that keeping an existing customer happy costs a company less than acquiring a new customer, and that losing a customer costs the company even more. A 1990 *Harvard Business Review* study revealed that reducing the number of customers lost by 5 percent can raise profits anywhere from 25 to 85 percent.

As the concept of customer service saturated business markets, many companies offered, as a selling point, "exemplary," "legendary," and "world-class" customer service, service that promised to not simply meet but to exceed customer expectations. The 1990s saw a glut of customer-service case studies and how-to books. Although the audience for such information was vast, those achieving results were few.

Aspects of Customer Service

The precepts of customer service have not changed greatly; the most basic version of customer service remains "service with a smile." Some businesses try to inspire loyalty with a so-called personal touch, which may involve calling a repeat customer by name or offering discounts to special customers. These small touches help businesses create a relationship with the customer. That relationship is often the only thing that keeps the customer from going to a competitor that offers lower prices.

Companies that excel at customer service have their own particular service styles. Southwest Airline's Customer Service Commitment reads, "We tell our Employees we are in the Customer Service business—we just happen to provide airline transportation." The idea that businesses are about service, regardless of the product, is echoed by many customer-service experts. Southwest further differentiated itself by hiring a team of flight attendants and phone operators who embody a specifically Southwest style of friendly irreverence.

Hiring and training is also a key practice for Federal Express, another company lauded for its customer service. FedEx developed standardized measures to test skills and abilities for its customer service

industries, many businesses still viewed them more as an obligation than as a business opportunity. Companies with a high level of customer service were often also the most successful—the most profitable. This realization led to a shift in business models, from one in which goods produced and services provided were considered business assets to one in which customers were also seen and valued as assets. Research has obs, including gauges for qualities like patience, judgment, initiative, and integrity. New hires are then given extensive training before being put to work. FedEx's dedication to internal customer service is often cited as a customer service best practice.

USAA, an insurance and financial services company for the U.S. military community, is similarly recognized as a high-level service provider. USAA developed a business practice called ECHO (Every Contact Has Opportunity), in which each phone call is used as an opportunity to develop a detailed picture of a customer and his or her current needs. Part of USAA's service, therefore, involves giving the customer someone to talk to. At the same time, the phone operator acts as a "listening post" for the company, which then uses the customer information to develop new products and services.

The Future of Customer Service

With the advent of the Internet, some aspects of customer service have changed. Online companies face ever-increasing demands for efficiency and, because of immense competition, enjoy fewer repeat customers than their real-world counterparts. In response, software developers have created various Customer Relationship Management (CRM) systems that store and manage information elements, including customer profiles and inventory levels, to meet the technological requirements of serving an online customer base.

Computers and networks have assisted businesses in rectifying a long-standing customer service problem—incomplete product and service records. Ideally, by consolidating records, any customer service representative within an organization has instant access to a customer's history, thus eliminating the need for repetitious, incomplete service, callbacks, and transfers.

Even as companies emulate the practices of FedEx, USAA, and highly regarded online service companies like Amazon.com, complaints about customer service remain high across the board. Customers still get

Nordstrom

For many years, Nordstrom, a family-run department store based in Seattle, was synonymous with excellent customer service. The company was noted for the quality of its sales staff and its generous return policy. Indeed, one of the most infamous Nordstrom customer service stories dates to the mid-1970s, when a salesperson allegedly refunded a customer the sales price of a car tire, even though Nordstrom had never carried tires in any of its stores.

Other anecdotes include a salesperson who, after failing to locate a particular size of sale-item pants in any Nordstrom store, went to a competing department store, bought the pants at full cost, and then sold the pants to the customer at the Nordstrom sale price. Such practices are generally considered anathema to the bottom line, but, by allowing sales staff such latitude, Nordstrom earned the loyalty of return customers and a powerful word-of-mouth reputation.

By 2000, Nordstrom sales had slipped because other aspects of its customer service—namely, the computer inventory system—lagged behind its competitors. Having since upgraded its technology, Nordstrom has been better able to deliver what Robert Spector, author of *The Nordstrom Way*, says is another major tenet of customer service—"the right merchandise and the right size and the right price at the right time."

lost in and frustrated with automated telephone services. Many call centers continue to lack adequate personnel. Most significant, the unpredictable human element of customer service—two personalities coming in contact—always remains. Customer service standards will continue to evolve as technology continues to transform business culture, and consumer advocates hope that more companies will implement the best practices for satisfying customers.

Further Reading

Benson, Susan Porter. *Counter Cultures: Saleswomen, Managers, and Customers in American Department Stores, 1890–1940.* Urbana: University of Illinois Press, 1988.

Blanchard, Kenneth, and Sheldon M. Bowles. *Raving Fan: A Revolutionary Approach to Customer Service.* New York: William Morrow, 1993.

Spector, Robert, and Patrick D. McCarthy. *The Nordstrom Way: The Inside Story of America's #1 Customer Service Company.* 2nd ed. New York: John Wiley & Sons, 2000.

Wiersema, Frederick, ed. *Customer Service: Extraordinary Results at Southwest Airlines, Charles Schwab, Lands' End, American Express, Staples, and USAA.* New York: HarperBusiness, 1998.

Zemke, Ron, and John A. Woods. *Best Practices in Customer Service.* New York: AMACOM, 1999.

—*Laura Lambert*

See also:
Credit History; Debt.

D&B

D&B, formerly Dun & Bradstreet, is the world's leading provider of information on the credit-worthiness of businesses. Because D&B specializes in collecting information on business firms, as opposed to individuals, it is also known as a mercantile agency. Such agencies provide their customers with ratings on a firm's financial condition, its operations, and credit history. In November 2001, Dun & Bradstreet officially changed its name to D&B.

D&B's origins date to the mid-nineteenth century, when Lewis Tappan founded the Mercantile Agency in New York in 1841. Born in 1788, Tappan was already a successful businessman when he lent his brother Arthur money to start a silk business in the 1820s. Tappan decided to enter the credit information business when the shortage of currency during the financial panic of 1837 wreaked havoc with his traditional cash-only policy on transactions. The Tappan brothers were hard-money men who disliked banks and credit, in part because little accurate financial information was available for businesses to evaluate the risks associated with extending credit. Tappan's goal in forming the Mercantile Agency was to create a clearinghouse for reliable and objective information on the creditworthiness of companies. In 1849, Tappan turned the agency over to Benjamin Douglass. Douglass worked to make the firm more professional by creating the position of credit reporter, a full-time employee skilled in the collection and interpretation of credit information.

In 1859, Robert Graham Dun took control of the Mercantile Agency, and, under its new name, R. G. Dun & Company, the company continued to expand operations so that by the end of the century it was a presence across the United States and in Europe. Dun's firm was not, however, the only major credit information business available. The John M. Bradstreet Company, formed in 1849, was an important rival, having popularized the use of credit ratings with publication of the first book of commercial ratings. Competition between the two firms continued until 1933 when the financial hardships of the Great Depression caused them to merge and form Dun & Bradstreet.

D&B currently gathers financial and statistical information on 70 million companies in 214 countries. This information comes from a variety of sources, including public records (court documents, government statistics, annual reports), media sources, and interviews with customers and company officials. Because of the scale of firms tracked and the scope of data collected by its reporters, D&B has developed a number of systems that have become standards in the credit industry. One such innovation is the Data Universal Numbering System (D&B D-U-N-S Number) used to identify businesses numerically for data-processing purposes. Each company

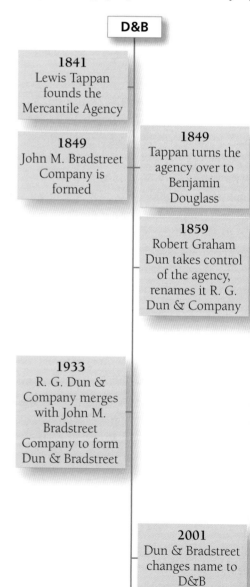

D&B

1841
Lewis Tappan founds the Mercantile Agency

1849
John M. Bradstreet Company is formed

1849
Tappan turns the agency over to Benjamin Douglass

1859
Robert Graham Dun takes control of the agency, renames it R. G. Dun & Company

1933
R. G. Dun & Company merges with John M. Bradstreet Company to form Dun & Bradstreet

2001
Dun & Bradstreet changes name to D&B

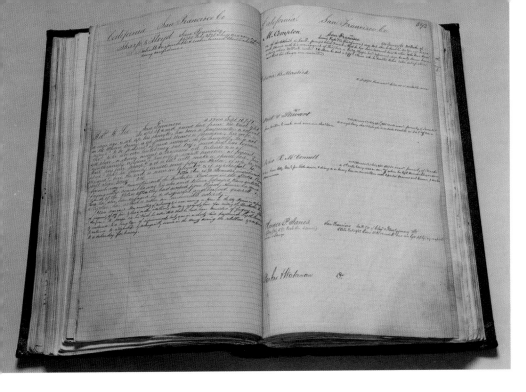

A ledger of the R. G. Dun Company, circa 1860s.

tracked by D&B is assigned a nine-digit number that provides unique identifiers of single business entities, while linking corporate family structures together. The D&B D-U-N-S Number has become a standard business identifier for the U.S. government, the United Nations, and the European Commission.

The raw company data are used to create several different reports for D&B customers. The basic document is the general business report that provides a summary of all aspects of a firm's operations. A typical general business report includes basic information (company address, products, key officers, financial statistics), with separate sections that describe a company's payment history to its customers, its banking relationships, its financial operations, history, and pending legal issues (if any). Other, more specialized, D&B reports provide detailed analysis of a company's credit risks based on its financial condition and operating history, as well as comparisons with similar firms.

Managers rely on D&B for a variety of purposes. Based on its reports, a company can manage business risks by being better able to predict the likelihood of a firm being delinquent or going bankrupt. D&B reports are also used to identify new business opportunities, improve existing customer relationships, and improve a firm's internal management systems. Finally, D&B products can be used by businesses seeking to expand into overseas markets or into e-commerce.

Further Reading

Foulke, Roy Anderson. *The Sinews of American Commerce*. New York: Dun & Bradstreet, Inc., 1941.

Newman, James Wilson. *Dun & Bradstreet, Established in 1841 for the Promotion and Protection of Trade*. New York: Newcomen Society in North America, 1956.

Norris, James D. *R.G. Dun & Co., 1841–1900: The Development of Credit-Reporting in the Nineteenth Century*. Westport, Conn.: Greenwood Press, 1978.

Young, Jeffrey, "Information Please." *Forbes*, 25 October 1993, 222–224.

—David Mason

Lewis Tappan: Businessman and Abolitionist

Lewis Tappan gave birth to the firm that became D&B; he was also involved in several social causes, including the abolition of slavery. Tappan supported the work of radical abolitionist William Lloyd Garrison, and Tappan's financial backing helped propel Garrison to national prominence. Both Lewis and his brother Arthur were members of Garrison's activist group, the American Anti-Slavery Society. The Tappan brothers would eventually disagree with Garrison's radicalism; the brothers founded their own group, the American and Foreign Anti-Slavery Society, in 1839. Their group advocated a political solution to the problem of slavery, evolving into the Liberty Party in 1840.

Tappan also brought the first civil rights case in U.S. history, *United States v. The Amistad*, to the attention of the national abolitionist movement. In 1841 Tappan raised most of the funds used to appeal this case, which involved a rebellion aboard the slave ship *The Amistad*, to the Supreme Court.

Data Management

Data and information are two terms that often are used interchangeably. They differ in meaning, however. Data are a series of characters and numbers; information is data that has meaning. Consider the following characters: GDX329. Someone just looking at this set of characters would not know what these letters and numbers signify. In this context, these characters would be data. If someone said that these letters and numbers represent a license plate number, the letters and numbers would take on meaning and become information.

As the use of technology by individuals, corporations, and nations continues to expand, the data that are collected will also grow significantly. A study released in 2000 by researchers at the University of California–Berkeley estimated that 1.5 billion gigabytes of information are created each year—the equivalent to every man, woman, and child on Earth churning out a novel the size of *Moby-Dick* each week.

Managing this vast and ever-expanding amount of data is a growing challenge. Professionals with data management skills like data administration, analysis, and mining, will always be in great demand.

Data management is the process of storing raw data in structured and easily retrievable formats. Tools used to store data include spreadsheets, databases, and data warehouses. Each of these solutions has varied degrees of complexity, usability, and functionality.

Spreadsheets

Spreadsheets are perhaps the easiest data management tools to use. Spreadsheets have features that allow users to change the format and manipulate the data easily. A spreadsheet can be readily converted to a graph, which allows the decision maker to visualize the information.

Typically, spreadsheets arrange data into a series of rows (horizontal lines), columns (vertical lines), and cells (intersections of rows and columns). Once numbers have been entered into the cells, a spreadsheet can add, subtract, multiply, divide, or perform many other numerical calculations.

The world of data management changed radically with personal computers. Previously, spreadsheets had to be created by hand and recalculated every time the data changed.

Because of their ability to perform calculations quickly, computer spreadsheets are most commonly used to track and record financial and accounting data. Many businesses as well as individuals use spreadsheets in their everyday activities. Popular spreadsheets on the market include Microsoft Excel, Lotus 1-2-3, and Quicken.

Database

A database is similar to an electronic filing system. While spreadsheets are designed to provide easy tools for storing and calculating data, databases focus on the ease of retrieving large amounts and varieties of information. While some databases provide a graphical user interface, most databases require written coded instructions to modify any database details. For this reason, individuals are not as likely to use databases as spreadsheets. Corporations, however, store most of their critical and everyday operational data in a database.

Three database models are available for managing corporate or personal data: hierarchical, network, and relational. Although all three models are used in organizations, the most popular model is the relational model. The relational model, proposed by E. F. Codd in 1970, applies concepts of relational algebra to the problem of storing large amounts of data. The relational model organizes data into tables that minimize data duplication and eliminate certain kinds of processing errors that occur when data are stored in other ways. If a company wants to store sales information by city and state, then city, state, and sales would each be separate tables in a relational database. Sales are associated with the city where they were made. Cities are associated with the state they are in. Therefore, sales would be connected to the individual states only through the city relationship.

Data Warehouse

A data warehouse is a more robust solution for retrieving and analyzing information. Data warehouses do not store up-to-the-minute transactions the way databases do.

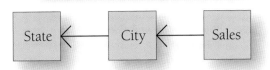

Rather, they store older data that a business considers critical to monitor and analyze.

The data in a data warehouse are often used in business reports and analyses. Users are able to search for any information they want without having to worry about slowing down or destroying the databases. A data warehouse has dimensions (typical search criteria) and facts (numerical, transactional-level details).

A data warehouse is usually organized by how the users will use the data and not necessarily by how the data are related. In the example of sales by city and state, state and city would both be dimension tables, and sales would be a fact table. In the diagram, the city and state values are directly linked to the sales table. The direct connection between the state and sales tables and between the city and sales tables reduces the time needed for the data warehouse to return search results. In this simplified example, the overall search time would not matter that much. However, a data warehouse usually contains hundreds of tables. Search times are dramatically improved by using a data warehouse rather than a relational database. Because of the complexity and cost involved in creating a data warehouse, data warehouse technology is generally used only by large businesses.

Impact of Data Management

The benefits of effective data management are enormous, but some problems still need

Effective data management is central to the success of an increasing number of companies. Here, an instructor teaches new employees how to use the company's data management software.

to be solved. A key issue will be how to manage the increasingly large amounts of scientific and technical data that are created and saved in digital data storage systems. This challenge is compounded by the increasing variety of formats in which data exists: strings of numbers, images, video, audio, arrays, graphics, algorithms, and documents.

Data mining is also part of data management. Often called knowledge discovery or pattern discovery, data mining is an effort to integrate various data sources that may be scattered across several sites and extract information from these data sources by locating patterns and trends that were previously unknown. The uses of data mining include providing information to improve marketing capabilities, detect abnormal

patterns, and predict future developments based on existing trends. For example, a supermarket could analyze the purchase record of its customers and, based on patterns the analysis shows, arrange items on shelves to improve sales. A credit bureau could analyze the credit history of its current or potential clients and find out which are higher risks. Physicians could analyze patient histories and current medical conditions and predict potential problems.

Despite its many uses, data mining could pose a threat to the security and privacy of individuals. For example, one controversial technique is called inference. Inference is the process by which users pose queries and make unwarranted assumptions from the legitimate responses they receive. Users with sophisticated tools can now access data and deduce patterns that could be sensitive. In addition, Web mining, which involves collecting data about the habits of people who use the World Wide Web, could potentially compromise the privacy of Web surfers.

Spreadsheets, databases, and data warehouses have all transformed the way people work. Tasks that used to take hours now take seconds. Data storage and retrieval tasks that were once impossible are relatively simple. Individuals can easily keep track of personal finances and budgets. Businesses can record and quickly access myriad details about their customers. Corporations can analyze their sales and more effectively forecast future sales patterns. Through proper organization, meaning becomes associated with the data in spreadsheets, databases, and data warehouses, transforming data into information.

Further Reading

Berry, Michael, and Gordon Linoff. *Mastering Data Mining: The Art and Science of Customer Relationship Management.* New York: Wiley Computer Pub., 2000.

Codd, E. F. "A Relational Model of Data for Large Shared Databanks." *Communications of the ACM* (June 1970): 377–387.

Stewart, Thomas A. *Intellectual Capital: The New Wealth of Organizations.* New York: Currency/Doubleday, 1997.

—Anil Kumar and Lacey Nimmer

Day Trading

Day trading involves trading stocks very quickly. Day traders try to pick up profits on fast-moving stocks, sometimes buying and selling shares of the same stock several times in the course of a day or a week. The best stocks for day trading are those that fluctuate in price a great deal, holding out the prospect of big gains in a single day. Generally, these are either very small and thinly traded stocks or, in many cases, Internet stocks. In fact, day traders control much of the daily trading action on the technology-heavy Nasdaq market and were one of the driving forces behind the wild fluctuations in Internet stock values during the late 1990s.

Internet technology also makes day trading possible. Using computer programs, day traders can buy and sell shares themselves, without the use of a broker. Internet brokerages reduce the cost of individual trades, and new computerized trading tools have made once-restricted market information available to everyone for a fee. The Internet also provides a network for the kind of instantaneous tips and rumors on which day trading relies.

Playing the Margins

Day traders make most of their money through small margins, that is, fluctuations in the price of a stock from one hour, or minute, to the next. If the price of a stock is moving up or down, a day trader can get between the bid price (what buyers are offering to pay for a stock) and the asked price (what stockholders are willing to sell for), then sell seconds later for a small profit per share. This kind of trade is often called a momentum play, and it takes split-second timing. A delay of a few minutes could cost traders all their profit.

Day traders rely completely on sophisticated Internet technology. Some day traders work from home, purchasing the programs themselves, but most work in day trading firms. In a firm, day traders pay a fee for the use of a desk, facilities,

secretaries, computers, connections to financial newswires, and Nasdaq Level II screens. A Level II screen shows the specific bid and asked prices in real time and the number of shares involved. Many Level II screens will also let traders bring up other real-time data, chart the recent price action of a stock, and graph the momentum and relative strength of the buying or selling pressure.

To begin trading, day traders put down an initial deposit of around $25,000 with the trade firm. They can also borrow money from the trading firm to purchase stock. The trading firm also takes a commission on every stock order.

Day Trading History

Day trading began in 1985, when Nasdaq's computerized Small Order Execution System (SOES) was created to allow trades of small amounts of stock. Many brokers at this time made money on the broker's spread; brokers would purchase stock for their clients at the buyer's bid price, then give the seller the asked price, and not the price they actually paid, which would be somewhere in the

See also:
Futures Markets; Nasdaq; New York Stock Exchange; Stocks and Bonds.

A sample Level II screen for a fictitious company. Level II screens are used by day traders to assess the sales pressure of a given stock; by looking at a Level II screen, traders can see who is looking to buy or sell a stock at any given moment.

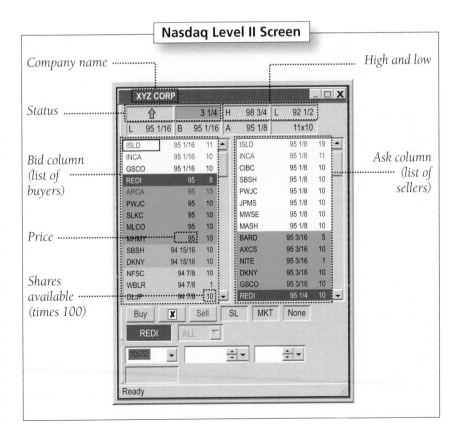

Nasdaq Level II Screen

Day traders discuss stock market information in 1998, in Boca Raton, Florida.

middle. A broker could do this because only the broker was able to move fast enough to take advantage of the small, rapid fluctuations between bid price and ask price.

Soon, day traders nicknamed "SOES bandits" began making large amounts of money using broker's spread techniques. In response, the National Association of Securities Dealers (NASD), which runs the Nasdaq stock market, fought to limit the use of SOES. In 1995 a court ruled that Nasdaq rules were unfair. The Securities and Exchange Commission issued rules forcing Nasdaq to strengthen SOES by increasing the number of shares available through SOES trading and the size of allowable trades.

At the same time, SOES trader Jeffrey Citron and computer programmer Josh Levine created a program that could automatically match bid and asked prices for all brokers, including those running day-trading rooms. The first of these programs was called "The Island," but many such programs, called Electronic Communication Networks (ECNs), are now available. By February 1998, ECNs were executing 22 percent of all Nasdaq trades.

Although day trading is becoming easier and more popular, it is also controversial.

Because day traders essentially take advantage of margins, they are not interested in owning a stock for its value, only for its possibility in moving up or down in price in the next few hours. Accordingly, day trading has been criticized as predatory and mercenary. As was the case with many Internet stocks, day trading can drive the price of stocks artificially high, giving a company a value it does not merit. In addition, many day traders become addicted to the fast pace. Many people have gone bankrupt by day trading. Because almost anyone can do it, those with no experience often find themselves beyond their expertise and heavily in debt.

Further Reading

Borsellino, Lewis J., with Patricia Commins. *The Day Trader: From the Pit to the PC.* New York: J. Wiley, 1999.

Deel, Robert. *The Strategic Electronic Day Trader.* New York: John Wiley & Sons, 2000.

Gonzalez, Fernando, and William Rhee. *Strategies for the Online Day Trader: Advanced Trading Techniques for Online Profits.* New York: McGraw-Hill, 1999.

Velez, Oliver, and Greg Capra. *Tools and Tactics for the Master Day Trader: Battle-Tested Techniques for Day, Swing, and Position Traders.* New York: McGraw-Hill, 2000.

—Lisa Magloff

Debt

Debt is a legal obligation to pay. A lender presumes that the debtor will enjoy a flow of cash in the future, that an indebted business will grow, and that investments will pay off. In the business world, debt involves using someone else's money to generate revenue with the intent to repay lenders and reward investors. This money can be used to fund the start of a business or expand an existing business. When debt is used constructively and managed properly, it can increase the value of a company over time.

Categories of Debt

However used, for start-up or expansion, debt falls into two broad categories: operating debt and investment debt. Operating debt is money borrowed to finance the daily or seasonal operation of a business. Investment debt pays for purchases like equipment, machinery, computers, and vehicles. Investment debt also includes payments made to bondholders—investors who have purchased promissory notes not secured by specific assets.

Individual debts can be short-term, as in commercial paper (30 to 90 days), which is used to fund inventory until it is sold, or long-term (years), often used to purchase office equipment or a building. Debts can be liquid or static. Liquid debts are those that can be converted to cash easily. For example, debt acquired from the purchase of office furniture is considered liquid because the furniture can be readily sold. Real estate and inventory are considered static.

Debt can be secured with assets, called collateral, or it can be unsecured. Examples of secured debt are mortgages and inventory stores. Examples of unsecured debt are bonds. Bonds are an investment in the business as a whole; therefore they are not tied to specific assets.

Debt Ratios and Cash Flow

Debt is a key element in the financial statements of a business. How debt falls on the balance sheet determines solvency, or whether a business has enough money to cover its debts. A balance sheet has two sides: liabilities (whatever takes money out of the business) and assets (whatever generates cash or retains value). Debt is a liability because money is going out of the business. If the debt is tied to a specific asset, the debt will show up on the liability side, and the amount of the asset that is paid for will show up on the asset side

See also:
Accounting and Bookkeeping; Cash Flow; Finance, Business; Finance, Personal; Inventory.

Analyzing Debt: Liquidity Ratios

- Liquidity ratios compare net worth to liabilities
- Liquidity ratios relate to ability to repay short-term debts
- The higher the ratio, the better the company is doing
- Banks are interested in the trend of these ratios over time
- Also of interest to short-term lenders like vendors and suppliers

Current Ratio

$$\frac{\text{Current assets}}{\text{Current liabilities}}$$

Company A

$$\frac{2,000,000}{1,000,000} = \text{2:1 (\$2.00 for every \$1 of debt)}$$

Company B

$$\frac{5,000,000}{4,000,000} = \text{1.25:1 (\$1.25 for every \$1 of debt)}$$

Both companies have $1 million of working capital; working capital equals current assets minus current liabilities. However, Company A has a better financial picture because it has a higher liquidity ratio.

Acid Test Ratio

- Eliminates least liquid assets, including inventories and prepaids

$$\frac{\text{Current assets} - \text{inventories and prepaids (expenses \& taxes)}}{\text{Current liabilities}}$$

Company A

$$\frac{2,000,000 - 800,000}{1,000,000} = 1.2:1$$

Company B

$$\frac{5,000,000 - 800,000}{4,000,000} = 1.05:1$$

However, when inventories and prepaids are taken into account, Company B is very close to Company A in its ability to pay its short-term debts.

- Debt ratios compare liabilities to other aspects of the financials
- Debt ratios relate to ability to repay long-term debts
- The lower the ratio, the better the company is doing
- Debt ratios are usually of interest to the company and its investors

Debt to Net Worth

$$\frac{\text{Total debt (current liabilities + long-term debt)}}{\text{Net worth}}$$

Company A

$$\frac{100{,}000 + 75{,}000}{225{,}000} \Bigg] \!\!-\!\! = 0.78{:}1$$

Company B

$$\frac{330{,}000 + 80{,}000}{500{,}000} \Bigg] \!\!-\!\! = 0.82{:}1$$

Debt to Total Capital

$$\frac{\text{Long-term debt}}{\text{Total capitalization (long-term debt + net worth)}}$$

Company A

$$\frac{75{,}000}{75{,}000 + 225{,}000} \Bigg] \!\!-\!\! = 0.25{:}1$$

Company B

$$\frac{80{,}000}{80{,}000 + 500{,}000} \Bigg] \!\!-\!\! = 0.14{:}1$$

Company B has a much better ratio when looking at total capital.

of the balance sheet. Traditional assets include real estate, inventory, furniture, fixtures, equipment, accounts receivable, and marketable securities.

Debt is weighed against various parts of the financial statement—operating expenses, interest, and taxes—to determine the ratio of debt in relation to assets, income potential, and equity. These ratios are called leverage ratios. Investors look at the leverage ratio to determine the viability of the company and the potential for return on their investment. A high ratio could mean that the business is about to go into default.

Other kinds of ratios are useful for debt management. Liquidity ratios give a point-in-time snapshot of a business's ability to convert assets into cash to cover its debts. Activity ratios are used to determine the rate of cash flow and are used to determine if a company generates enough cash to pay its obligations. Profitability ratios compare different categories in the balance sheet to determine how efficiently a company generates profits. Some of these comparisons will indicate whether a company is carrying too many assets or too much inventory, even if the company is profitable in general. Too many assets or inventory indicate that money is sitting idle and could be used elsewhere to generate more profit.

Business owners, lenders, and investors use debt information to determine risk and to monitor their investments. By analyzing the ratios, accountants can tell how well a business is doing at any point in time. When debt ratios are out of proportion on the negative side, the company may have problems meeting its financial obligations. If investors and lenders are not willing to bail the company out, a business may shut down or file for bankruptcy. Bankruptcy may include a pardon of debts or a restructuring of the debt to pay it back on different terms than originally agreed to.

Claims Structure

Debt gives lenders and investors a claim on the business's income and assets when a company cannot meet its financial obligations. One consideration in taking on debt is the claim structure of the lenders and investors. This structure is especially important to understand if the bondholders are family and friends who invested because of personal relationships.

Creditors have the first claim on income and assets. Those debts secured with specific assets give the lender specific claims. For example, a mortgage or debts to a vendor for special equipment are considered creditors with specific claims. This kind of lender typically plays no role in management when something goes wrong. They simply repossess their asset. Some creditors, for example, bondholders, have a general claim. Bonds

Purpose of Debt Held by Families 1998

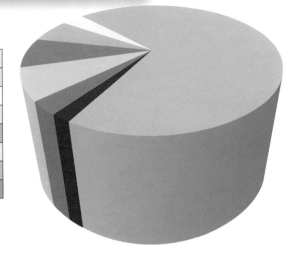

Home purchase	68.1%
Other loans	2.0%
Education	3.4%
Goods and services	6.0%
Vehicles	7.5%
Investment (real estate)	7.8%
Investment (excluding real estate)	3.2%
Home improvement	2.0%

Source: Federal Reserve, *Federal Reserve Bulletin,* 2000.

The vast majority of debt held by American families relates to home ownership; a mortgage is considered good debt because property gains value over time.

are not tied to specific items in the business. Bondholders can step into a management role in the case of problems with payment.

Stockholders have second and third claim to income and assets. Preferred stockholders have second claim; common stockholders have third claim. Although creditors and preferred stockholders have a higher claim on assets, common stockholders usually make more money on return on investments when the company prospers.

Alternatives to Debt

Often a business needs to avoid debt yet needs more capital to grow or fund research and development. The various alternatives all need to be balanced against cash flow, tax implications, time commitment to secure the funds, and existing debt structure.

One option for obtaining furniture, fixtures, and equipment is lease financing. For example, a business may choose to lease computer equipment with the option to buy at the end of the lease. The issue here is ownership. As of 1987, if a leasing company includes an option to buy in the lease, then it is treated as a traditional loan in which the business leasing the equipment owns the equipment. If that clause is not included, then the leasing company retains ownership. Although the equipment will end up costing more than if bought with a traditional loan, the business gains the advantage of having the lease listed as a liability, but not as a debt.

The same advantage exists with renting versus owning real estate. A rental lease is a liability, but not a debt. A mortgage is a debt where the business retains ownership of the property and all its inherent liabilities. Once again, the issue is ownership: a mortgage, over time, leads to a substantial asset. However, if a company is already near its debt limit, then renting is a good option.

Another option is bartering. With bartering, a business will exchange its goods or services for the goods or services of another business. For example, a graphics firm could produce made-to-order advertising materials for a builder in exchange for carpentry work. This transaction has tax implications and must be recorded as if it occurred in cash. The taxes related to the transaction may actually need to be paid in cash to make bartering worthwhile. Businesses that barter can be found through trade associations or the local chamber of commerce. Professional bartering associations charge a fee for providing the point of contact between the parties.

Grants, tax credits, and venture capital are also viable options for raising capital without going into debt. Federal and state grants are available to some kinds of businesses and some industries. Competition is intense for limited funds, so much time and effort must be expended to win grant

Unsecured consumer debt—money owed to credit card companies—is considered bad debt because it lowers a person's net worth. High levels of consumer debt can cause stress if more money is going out than is coming in.

money. Some companies use professional grant writers to write the proposals and fill out the paperwork. Some cities, counties, or states offer businesses tax credits for locating in a particular area, for example, in an inner-city revival area. If a company has a product that is unique or on the cutting edge of science, medicine, or technology, it may be a candidate for venture capital. During the 1990s, many Internet start-ups ran on venture capital.

Partnerships can be used to steer clear of debt, too. A limited partnership has a silent partner who puts up money but leaves the business side alone. A limited partner will expect a return on the investment in the form of dividends.

Business versus Personal Debt

In business, debt is considered normal. It can be used to start a business, to expand it, for capital improvements, for inventory, and for many other reasons. From a tax standpoint, debt is desirable because the interest is tax deductible, whereas equity is taxed. Business owners are accountable to their lending institutions and investors for the amount of debt they incur in relation to the value of their business. They constantly monitor their debt against their assets to maintain solvency.

Personal debt has some similarity to business debt. Personal debt falls into many of the same categories as business debt, including long-term or short-term, liquid or illiquid, secured or unsecured. As with businesses, some kinds of personal debt, such as a home mortgage, can be economically wise in the long run.

However, many consumers get into trouble with debt when they overextend themselves in the area of unsecured consumer debt—that is, with credit cards. Credit purchases of consumable goods that retain little or no value once purchased are a major departure from business debt. Credit card debt is rarely used to increase a person's net worth, whereas in business the idea is to use debt to increase the value of the business and make a profit.

Further Reading

Heath, Gibson. *Getting the Money You Need: Practical Solutions for Financing Your Small Business.* Chicago: Irwin Professional Publishing, 1995.

Siegel, Joel G., and Jae K. Shim. *Keys to Managing Your Cash Flow.* New York: Barron's, 1992.

—*Stephanie Buckwalter*

Deere, John

1804–1886
Founder of Deere & Company

In pushing forward the boundaries of the American frontier, settlers risked their lives and fortunes moving westward, drawn by the promise of inexpensive farmland. John Deere was one of those settlers; he was also an inventor and entrepreneur.

Deere was born in Rutland, Vermont, in 1804. His parents were poor and encouraged him to become a blacksmith because they hoped that having a specialized skill would lead to financial security. He spent several years as an apprentice, becoming a journeyman in 1825.

Deere soon gained a reputation as a skilled smith, producing tools like hay-forks and shovels for the farmers in western Vermont. Financial success eluded him, however. His first business burned down in a fire, and then Vermont experienced an economic downturn in the middle of the 1830s. In 1836 Deere sought new opportunities; hearing of the village of Grand Detour, Illinois, which had been settled by Vermonters, Deere left Vermont and moved to Illinois, where he was able to start his own business immediately because blacksmiths were in great demand on the frontier.

Initially he produced the standard goods—horseshoes and other products needed by the local farmers—but Deere quickly realized that he had a tremendous opportunity. The local farmland was fertile but was too heavy for the plows the Vermonters had brought with them. The dirt stuck to the plows, forcing the farmers to stop frequently to clean them. This made farming difficult and led many to complain about their equipment.

Deere found his solution in a sawmill in 1836. He had repaired a piece of equipment for the owner and noticed a broken saw blade. Deere took the blade home and crafted a plow from it. The new tool was a tremendous success. The sawtooth edge easily broke through the earth without the heavy soil sticking to it. Tilling the soil became less arduous and agriculture began to thrive in local conditions.

From this point on, Deere was in the plow business. He had to overcome significant obstacles to make his business a success. One problem was the lack of polished steel available to make the plows. Deere begun to import the steel to Illinois, initially from England and later from

See also:
Agriculture Industry.

An undated portrait of John Deere.

Deere's Gilpin Sulky Plow breaks the earth with a three-horse team as Deere observes.

Pittsburgh. Another problem was that transportation of heavy equipment to Illinois was hampered by a lack of roads or railroads. The first loads of steel had to travel first by river, then by wagon, to reach Deere's factory, adding to his costs and reducing his ability to sell his plows. Deere moved his operations to Moline, Illinois, on the banks of the Mississippi River.

The growth of Deere's company was further hampered by competition and legal problems. In the nineteenth century, manufacturers commonly borrowed ideas from competitors to improve their products. Deere did produce the first polished plow; however, it is uncertain how many other improvements were his. He was plagued by frequent lawsuits that distracted him from his business.

In Moline, Deere found a temporary solution by taking on several new business partners. They provided additional money and the bookkeeping expertise Deere lacked, allowing him to focus on product development and sales. Production and sales rose. Unfortunately, credit problems led to the dissolution of the partnership.

Deere struck out under his own name in 1858, with his son Charles joining the business that same year. From that point

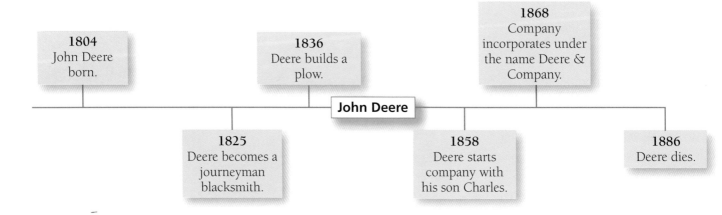

1804
John Deere born.

1825
Deere becomes a journeyman blacksmith.

1836
Deere builds a plow.

John Deere

1858
Deere starts company with his son Charles.

1868
Company incorporates under the name Deere & Company.

1886
Deere dies.

Deere & Company's
7000 series tractors.

the company grew because of a combination of effective marketing and continued innovation. For example, John Deere products were featured at county fairs. Competitions for farming equipment were held as a way for farmers to easily compare products. Deere's products frequently won, greatly helping sales. The firm was incorporated as Deere & Company in 1868.

Deere's career ended abruptly. He was forced to give up control of his company to avoid a personal bankruptcy. His son Charles took over and led the company to prosperity during the economic boom caused by the Civil War. Deere & Co. is still in business today, a monument to frontier determination and endurance, 180 years after Deere first began producing farm implements. John Deere now sells tools not only to farmers but also to loggers, gardeners, groundskeepers, and even golf courses all over the world.

Further Reading

Beemer, Rod, and Chester Peterson, Jr. *Inside John Deere: A Factory History.* Osceola, Wis.: MBI Publishing, 1999.
Broehl, Wayne G., Jr. *John Deere's Company: A History of Deere & Company and Its Times.* New York: Doubleday, 1984.

—David Long

See also:
Dow Chemical Company;
Research and Development;
Sikorsky, Igor.

Defense Industry

The day a cave dweller first picked up a rock to defend the home turf could be considered the unofficial beginning of the defense industry. Although the industry has come a long way from rocks, the guiding principle remains the same: defense of territory, either at home, or, if national interests dictate, abroad.

After the terrorist attacks of September 11, 2001, the U.S. defense industry, which had seen a reduction in output at the end of the cold war, experienced renewed growth. In 1999, U.S. military expenditures were estimated at approximately $276 billion. With expenditures for defense estimated to be close to $400 billion in 2002, appropriations for this industry are taking an increasing percentage of the U.S. budget.

Recent History of the Defense Industry
Although two Americans, the Wright brothers, were the first to take to the air, the Europeans dominated the world market in the early years of airplane manufacture. World War I brought about change: When the United States entered that war in 1916, the country became a major military power.

Prior to World War I, neither the U.S. Army nor the U.S. Navy had played a significant role in foreign policy. The army served primarily to enforce America's notion of manifest destiny, the belief that U.S. borders were preordained (possibly by God) to stretch from the Atlantic to the Pacific and beyond. The navy ensured that U.S. business interests were protected during the colonial scramble of the nineteenth century.

Elihu Root, appointed secretary of war during the administration of President William McKinley, created in the early years of the twentieth century the foundations for America's current role as superpower and global police officer. Root quadrupled the size of the standing army; established federal command over the National Guard; created officer training colleges; and, in 1903, established the Joint Chiefs of Staff to act as military advisers to the secretary of war. (The position of secretary of war was later renamed secretary of defense.)

As the making of war depends on the making of weaponry, and weaponry is linked to technological changes, the technological developments of the late nineteenth and early twentieth centuries would ultimately make modern warfare possible. The growth of the petroleum industry, advances in the steel, rubber, and chemical industries, and mass production prior to World War I made possible both victory and the war's massive destruction. Mustard gas, made by Dow Chemical and others and used during World War I, was a precursor to modern chemical and biological weapons. Handheld weapons became more lethal, ships larger and faster, and, for the first time, armored tanks rumbled across the land.

These changes enabled the United States to make a brief and decisive entry into World War I. World War II enabled the U.S. defense industry to become the world's major manufacturer and exporter of missiles, bombers, jets, personnel carriers, warships, and other implements of warfare. In

In the 1940s, cannons left over from World War I were melted down and reused to make munitions for World War II.

1943, 1,345,600 persons worked in the production of military aircraft in the United States. That year, the defense industry was America's major employer.

Following World War II, the cold war ushered in a new period of growth for the defense industry. The space program was also influenced by the cold war. In 1957 the United States undertook a massive effort to catch up with the Soviets, who that year had launched the *Sputnik* satellite.

The first intercontinental ballistic missile (ICBM) program, begun in the early 1950s, brought a host of changes to the industry, with Lockheed Missiles & Space taking the lead in ICBM production. Instead of the giant buildings required to assemble aircraft, smaller factories became the norm. The cutting-edge technology demanded by the new missiles proved attractive to a generation of young engineers who flocked to join the ranks of defense industry innovators.

The Military–Industrial Complex

As President Dwight D. Eisenhower's term drew to a close in 1961, the defense industry was witnessing an unprecedented expansion of government financing and support. Private and public colleges as well as politicians were getting involved in a massive shift that would eventually see a growing portion of the nation's budget dedicated to military expenditures. With government agencies offering generous funding for academic research, with politicians eager to get defense dollars funneled into their states, and with the number of contracts between the armed forces and private industries increasing, the links among the military, universities, politicians, and private industry were becoming firmly established and increasingly intricate.

The expansion of the U.S. defense industry was jump-started by Russia's successful launch of the Sputnik I *satellite. Here, technicians at the Moscow Planetarium plot the orbit of the satellite in October 1957.*

A worker in San Jose, California, inspects personnel carriers in the final construction phase before they are shipped to Egypt.

In the course of delivering his farewell address, Eisenhower warned of the "unwarranted influence" of a powerful "military-industrial complex," a term for the interconnections between the U.S. economy and its military. Eisenhower said, "Only an alert and knowledgeable citizenry can compel the proper meshing of the huge industrial and military machinery of defense with our peaceful methods and goals, so that security and liberty may prosper together."

During the Vietnam War, which came under increasing criticism, many decried the undue influence of the military-industrial complex on American politics, economics, and society. At the same time, it is worth noting that this era saw the creation of the Internet, which, for a time, was entirely supported by a triangle of military, corporate, and university resources.

Military expenditures continued to increase throughout the 1970s and rose precipitously during the 1980s. Between 1980 and 1989, during the administration of President Ronald Reagan, the military-industrial complex again came under fire after a period of increased defense spending, nuclear weapons buildup, and U.S. military involvement around the globe.

When the administration's sometimes clandestine support of the counterrevolutionary Contras in Nicaragua with arms and money became known, significant protests followed. Another outcry followed Reagan's proposal for a missile-defense program based on missiles orbiting Earth (dubbed "Star Wars" by the media). The plan was eventually abandoned but not entirely forgotten by either defense contractors or the Pentagon; the military continues to test a related system known as the Strategic Defense Initiative.

Careers in the Defense Industry

The role played by the United States as the world's only superpower suggests that the defense industry will be looking for more than a few good men and women to fill its ranks. Job openings and opportunities for graduate study following college appear to be growing.

Lockheed Martin, which in October 2001 won a Pentagon contract for a new fighter jet, Tecolote Research, Northrop Grumman, and Raytheon are among the industry leaders that plan to increase their hires. Engineers are in particular demand, though factory workers employed on the line will also be needed. According to the Department of Labor Statistics, employment opportunities for engineers are expected to remain strong until at least 2008.

For those interested in a career in aerospace or the defense industry, a solid background in math and science is highly recommended. Advanced courses in calculus, trigonometry, and physics should be part of the curriculum. Many postgraduate programs are available for both undergraduates and graduate students. In addition, some agencies, including NASA, offer grants for postgraduate study.

The Contemporary Defense Industry

Following the collapse of the Soviet Union and the end of the cold war, the defense industry underwent still another change. By 1995 only 4.3 percent of those employed in manufacturing were working for the aerospace industry, down from 8.8 percent in 1989. A period of

consolidations and mergers followed. General Electric sold its aerospace division to Martin Marietta, which in turn was purchased by Lockheed to become Lockheed Martin. Boeing acquired Rockwell International and McDonnell Douglas. In 1997 Raytheon purchased Hughes Electronics.

In August 1997 Boeing merged with the McDonnell Douglas Corporation. Following the merger, major development programs included the International Space Station, the F-22 Raptor fighter, the F/A-18 Super Hornet, the Joint Strike Fighter, the Delta group of launch vehicles, C-17 Globemaster III missiles, Global Positioning System satellites, Airborne Warning and Control System aircraft, and the AH-64 Apache Longbow.

At the turn of the twentieth century, three manufacturers led the list of defense contractors. Lockheed Martin, Boeing, and

Raytheon won national defense contracts for $15.1, $12, and $6.3 million, respectively. Lockheed Martin's main products include a full range of space launch systems, ground systems, remote sensing and communications satellites, advanced space observatories, spacecraft, ballistic missiles, and missile defense systems.

Complex Controversies

Over the years, the U.S. military–industrial complex has provided billions of dollars in arms to nations around the world. This controversial policy has resulted in the United States finding itself in the position of supplying arms to nations it may deem an ally at one time and an enemy at another.

For example, in the 1980s the United States helped arm resistance fighters in Afghanistan who were trying to repel a

A Patriot missile launch at the White Sands Missile Range, New Mexico.

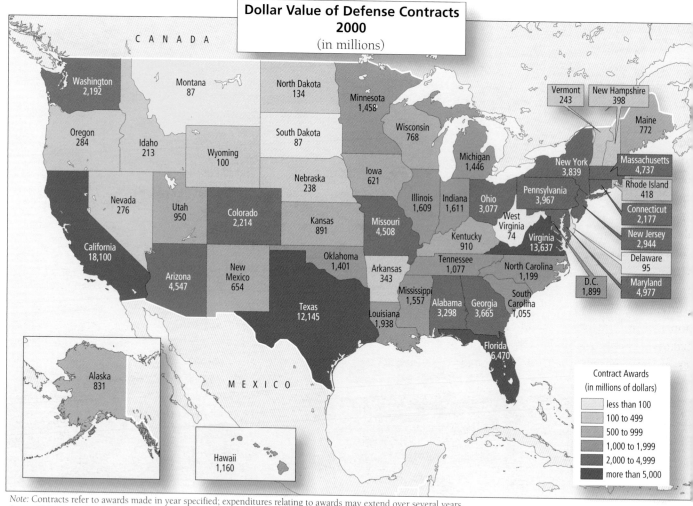

Dollar Value of Defense Contracts 2000
(in millions)

CANADA

Washington 2,192
Montana 87
North Dakota 134
Minnesota 1,458
Vermont 243
New Hampshire 398
Maine 772
Oregon 284
Idaho 213
Wyoming 100
South Dakota 87
Wisconsin 768
Michigan 1,446
New York 3,839
Massachusetts 4,737
Rhode Island 418
Nevada 276
Utah 950
Colorado 2,214
Nebraska 238
Iowa 621
Illinois 1,609
Indiana 1,611
Ohio 3,077
Pennsylvania 3,967
Connecticut 2,177
California 18,100
Kansas 891
Missouri 4,508
Kentucky 910
West Virginia 74
Virginia 13,637
New Jersey 2,944
Delaware 95
Arizona 4,547
New Mexico 654
Oklahoma 1,401
Arkansas 343
Tennessee 1,077
North Carolina 1,199
D.C. 1,899
Maryland 4,977
Texas 12,145
Mississippi 1,557
Alabama 3,298
Georgia 3,665
South Carolina 1,055
Louisiana 1,938
Florida 6,470

Alaska 831

MEXICO

Hawaii 1,160

Contract Awards
(in millions of dollars)
less than 100
100 to 499
500 to 999
1,000 to 1,999
2,000 to 4,999
more than 5,000

Note: Contracts refer to awards made in year specified; expenditures relating to awards may extend over several years.
Source: U.S. Dept. of Defense, *Atlas/Data Abstract for the United States and Selected Areas,* annual.

The economies of many states depend on defense contracts from the U.S. government.

Soviet invasion. After the defeat of the Soviets, some of the resistance fighters joined the Taliban regime, which became a target of the U.S. war on terrorism in 2001. Also in the 1980s, the United States helped arm Iraq in its war against Iran; in the next decade the United States went to war against Iraq and led the calls for international sanctions against that nation. In some instances, the Pentagon brokers these deals between the United States and other countries. In other cases, arms manufacturers, after receiving a license from the State Department, may negotiate directly with a purchasing nation.

As the United States entered the twenty-first century with the largest military budget of any nation in history and its role as superpower secure, the warnings of Eisenhower may seem very far away. Some would argue,

however, that with the renewed national focus on defense, the sharp increase in military spending, and the proliferation of weapons of mass destruction, his words are more relevant than ever.

Further Reading

Bilstein, Roger E. *The American Aerospace Industry: From Workshop to Global Enterprise.* New York: Twayne Publisher, 1996.

Koistinen, Paul A. C. *The Military–Industrial Complex: A Historical Perspective.* New York: Praeger, 1980.

Pattillo, Donald M. *Pushing the Envelope: The American Aircraft Industry.* Ann Arbor: University of Michigan Press, 1998.

Perret, Geoffrey. *A Country Made by War: From the Revolution to Vietnam—the Story of America's Rise to Power.* New York: Random House, 1989.

Vander Meulen, Jacob. *The Politics of Aircraft: Building an American Military Industry.* Lawrence: University Press of Kansas, 1991.

—*Connie Tuttle*

Demographics

Demographics describe the characteristics of a specific population, using such categories as age, income, sex, education, geographic location, and so on. The baby boom generation, for instance, is a demographic group comprising individuals born between 1946 and 1964, a generation that came of age during the turbulence of the 1960s and the Vietnam War. The baby boomers make up almost 30 percent of the U.S. population.

Demographics play a pivotal role in marketing strategies for businesses. Companies spend much of their financial resources studying a demographic group in the hopes of fulfilling its consumer needs. For example, prompted by demographic studies of their fans, in the mid-1990s major sports organizations, which had largely ignored the female market in the past, launched advertising and marketing campaigns to introduce women's apparel. Retail sales of women's sports apparel in 1996 were $13.2 billion, with women accounting for 36 percent of the $12 billion athletic footwear market.

Women are not the only consumer demographic group to be targeted. American teenagers, sometimes referred to by marketers as Generation Y, constitute an even more powerful demographic, with tremendous spending potential. A study by Teenage Research Unlimited revealed that young adults aged 12 to 19 spent $172 billion in the year 2001 alone. This marks a 1.3 percent spending increase compared with 1999, and these figures are expected to continue to rise. A huge variety of businesses

See also:
Advertising, Business Practice; Immigration; Public Relations and Marketing, Business Practice.

Teenage shoppers are a key demographic group for many industries, including fashion and music.

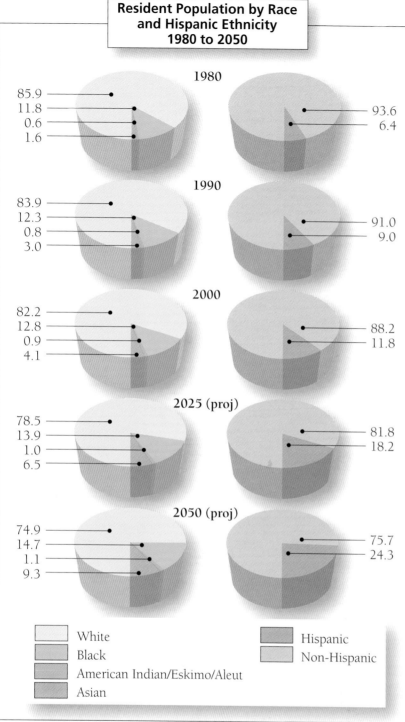

Resident Population by Race and Hispanic Ethnicity 1980 to 2050

1980
85.9
11.8
0.6
1.6

93.6
6.4

1990
83.9
12.3
0.8
3.0

91.0
9.0

2000
82.2
12.8
0.9
4.1

88.2
11.8

2025 (proj)
78.5
13.9
1.0
6.5

81.8
18.2

2050 (proj)
74.9
14.7
1.1
9.3

75.7
24.3

White
Black
American Indian/Eskimo/Aleut
Asian

Hispanic
Non-Hispanic

Note: Persons of Hispanic ethnicity may be of any race.
Source: Statistical Abstracts, 2001.

various demographic categories. For example, in the late 1990s Nike conducted a targeted marketing campaign to reach young, urban, southern California consumers with a specific interest in extreme and alternative sports. The more specific the demographic, the more customized the marketing strategies must and can be.

Demographics are not static. The desires of demographic groups change—what young, urban, southern Californians are shopping for today may not be what they shop for tomorrow. Similarly, as the powerful baby boom demographic continues to age, the products and services they seek will shift. Furthermore, demographic groups are themselves always subtly shifting. Businesses that sell products directly to consumers invest significantly in demographic research because keeping abreast of these delicate shifts is key to success.

Demographic Shifts in the United States
The United States is experiencing dramatic demographic changes. Projections show that by the middle of the twenty-first century, the United States will be a pluralistic nation in which no racial group is in the majority. Even more significant than population growth will be the cumulative effects of immigration. By 2050 the U.S. population will include 82 million people who arrived in or were born to people who arrived in the country after 1991. This group of immigrants and their children will account for 21 percent of America's population. These demographic changes are certain to profoundly affect the way business is conducted.

Unlike the immigrants of the nineteenth century, contemporary ethnic minority immigrants often attempt to maintain their cultural identities. They are slower to assimilate into mainstream American culture compared with their earlier counterparts. The view of the United States as one giant melting pot has given way to a vision of a quilt of varied American cultures. Businesses will have to employ distinct regional and ethnic marketing strategies to

have attempted to capitalize on the teen market, ranging from specialty magazines like *Sports Illustrated for Kids* to clothing lines, from teen-targeted snack foods to boy bands.

In addition to studying specific age or gender demographics, businesses, in an attempt to tailor a product to consumers, may conduct market research that combines

sell their products to an increasingly diverse population base.

In addition, businesses will have to be attentive to a changed and changing labor pool: everyone will belong to a minority group. White men will constitute less than half of the labor force; more than one employee in four will come from an ethnic minority group. Hispanics will far outstrip other groups as the nation's largest minority, and immigrants will become more important to U.S. population growth than natural increase. Using the right products and messages will be imperative when targeting these diverse groups.

The American family underwent profound changes in the second half of the twentieth century, and this trend is expected to continue well into the twenty-first century. Full-time homemakers will approach extinction as more than 80 percent of women age 25 to 54 will be in the labor force, and most children will never know a time when their mothers did not work outside the home. Businesses and other institutions will be increasingly dependent upon women's skills and will have to adapt to keep them on the job. Parental leave and child care at the workplace are expected to eventually become the norm for all but the smallest organizations.

In addition, business will have to reorient its view of the traditional family. Married couples will no longer constitute a majority of households, and more than half of all children will spend part of their lives in single-parent homes. By 2010 about one in three married couples with children will have a stepchild or an adopted child. Nontraditional family structures will become more prevalent, including unmarried heterosexual couples, homosexual couples, and friends who live together. As a consequence, businesses will have to become increasingly tactful in characterizing family life in advertising, on product packaging, and in marketing efforts.

Further Reading

Chideya, Farai. *The Color of Our Future*. New York: William Morrow, 1999.

Johnson, James H., Jr., Walter C. Farrell, Jr., and Chandra Guinn. "Immigration Reform and the Browning of America: Tensions, Conflicts, and Community Instability in Los Angeles." In *The Handbook of International Migration*. Edited by Charles Hirschman, Phillip Kasinitz, and Josh DeWind. New York: Russell Sage Foundation, 1999.

Russell, Cheryl. *Demographics of the U.S.: Trends and Projections*. Ithaca, N.Y.: New Strategist Publications, 2000.

—Walter C. Farrell, Jr., Renée Sartin Kirby, and Nicole Cohen

Deregulation

During the last quarter of the twentieth century, the United States and other nations of the world moved to reduce government influence on their economies. This was accomplished in several ways—by turning government enterprises over to private companies and by reducing or rethinking prior commitments to government regulation.

That trend toward deregulation is often associated with the rise to power of two conservatives—Margaret Thatcher, who became prime minister of England in 1979, and Ronald Reagan, who was elected president of the United States in 1980. In fact, however, the trend began in 1977, when Democratic president Jimmy Carter asked Alfred Kahn, a Cornell University professor, to head the Civil Aeronautics Board (CAB), which regulated airlines.

Conservative Republicans had long opposed regulation, taking their lead from free-market economists like Milton Friedman, Friedrich von Hayek, and George Stigler at the University of Chicago. Kahn was not part of that conservative school. He was a liberal, and a follower of Thorstein Veblen, the satirical writer and economist whose work *The Theory of the Leisure Class* (1899) was sharply skeptical about the ability of the free market to deliver the greatest happiness to the most people.

Kahn was also a realist. What he found in Washington was a growing political consensus that airline regulation had failed. The CAB had been established during the 1930s, near the beginning of the Great Depression, and was supposed to ensure reliable service and low rates for airline customers. By 1977, however, many analysts had concluded that regulation was not benefiting consumers; rather, it was protecting inefficient and poorly run airlines. Support for deregulating the airlines was growing even among liberal Democrats, including Senator Ted Kennedy of Massachusetts, who was being advised on regulatory matters by Stephen Breyer, a lawyer who later was named to the U.S. Supreme Court. "The CAB was supposed to be protecting the public," Breyer said. "But regulation was leading to higher prices. [The CAB] spent 95 percent of its time keeping prices from being too low instead of pushing them to get lowered."

At first, Kahn moved slowly to lift the regulations on airline schedules and fares. He concluded, however, that gradual deregulation did not work, and he moved to eliminate airline regulation altogether. The result was an upheaval in the industry; in the aftermath, companies like Pan American Airlines and Eastern Airlines went out of business. Prices fell, however, and competition increased. America became a nation of fliers, with the number of passengers more than doubling in the next two decades.

Over the course of the next quarter-century, deregulation spread to the trucking industry, the telecommunications industry, the health care industry, the electric power industry, and many others. Regulations were removed, competition was encouraged, and the reach of what eighteenth-century economist Adam Smith called the "invisible hand" of the free market extended further than ever.

President Jimmy Carter signs legislation deregulating the airline industry.

Deregulation of AT&T

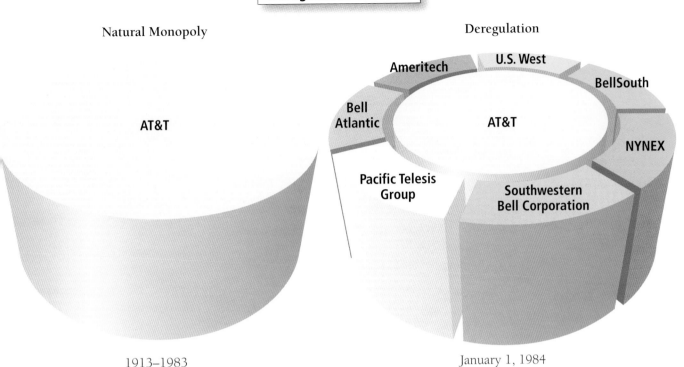

Natural Monopoly

AT&T

1913–1983

Deregulation

Ameritech · U.S. West · BellSouth · Bell Atlantic · AT&T · NYNEX · Pacific Telesis Group · Southwestern Bell Corporation

January 1, 1984

The shape of AT&T, before and after the company breakup.

The deregulatory movement in the United States was influential elsewhere, as several nations moved to sell off government-owned businesses and reduce the burden of government regulation. The collapse of the Soviet Union in the late 1980s eliminated communism as an alternative model for government's role in the economy. The failure of the Japanese economy in the 1990s, as well as the Asian economic crisis of 1997, undercut any idea that the Asian model of economic development, in which governments helped to guide business investment, might be superior to the capitalism of the United States. By the end of the twentieth century, except in isolated areas remaining committed to collectivist ideologies, only one model for a successful economy remained: the market economy with limited government intervention.

A Legacy of the Progressive Era

Government regulation of the economy in the United States dates to the end of the nineteenth century, when a progressive Congress established the Interstate Commerce Commission to regulate the railroads. In the Great Depression and the years that followed, government regulation was expanded to the airlines, telephone companies, and other areas. Economists focused their attention on the failures of the marketplace. Whenever a market failure was found, a government regulatory solution was proposed.

By the 1970s, however, a growing group of economists had concluded that, although the free market sometimes failed to serve society's needs, so, too, did government regulation. In many cases, as in the case of the CAB, a regulated industry would "capture" the regulator with skillful lobbying; then it would use the regulatory regime to its own advantage, rather than to the advantage of consumers. Nobel Prize–winning economist George Stigler was one of the first to explain this sad cycle, but he persuaded others. Liberals, including Alfred Kahn and Stephen Breyer, joined their conservative brethren in opposing regulation.

Economist Lawrence Summers (treasury secretary under President Bill Clinton) told Daniel Yergin the story of his own conversion. Yergin wrote a book on the global trend toward deregulation, *The Commanding Heights* (1998), and included the Summers conversation. Summers said his parents, both

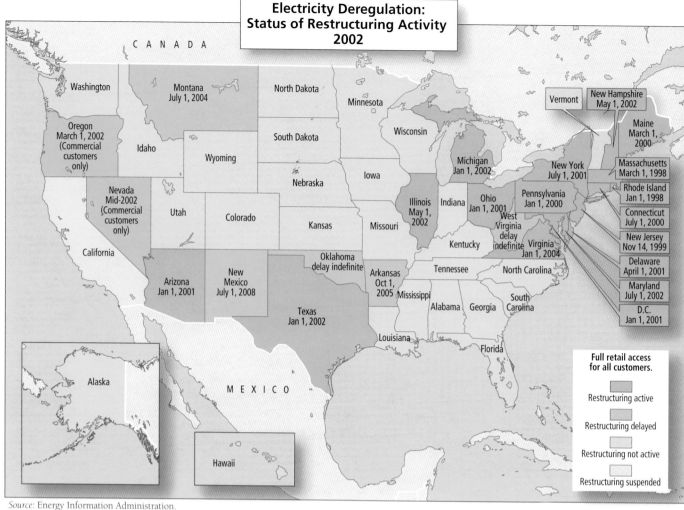

Electricity Deregulation: Status of Restructuring Activity 2002

CANADA

Washington

Montana
July 1, 2004

North Dakota

Minnesota

Vermont

New Hampshire
May 1, 2002

Oregon
March 1, 2002
(Commercial
customers
only)

Idaho

South Dakota

Wisconsin

Maine
March 1,
2000

Nevada
Mid-2002
(Commercial
customers
only)

Wyoming

Nebraska

Iowa

Michigan
Jan 1, 2002

New York
July 1, 2001

Massachusetts
March 1, 1998

Rhode Island
Jan 1, 1998

Utah

Colorado

Illinois
May 1,
2002

Indiana

Ohio
Jan 1, 2001

Pennsylvania
Jan 1, 2000

Connecticut
July 1, 2000

New Jersey
Nov 14, 1999

California

Kansas

Missouri

West
Virginia
delay
indefinite

Virginia
Jan 1, 2004

Kentucky

Delaware
April 1, 2001

Maryland
July 1, 2002

Arizona
Jan 1, 2001

New
Mexico
July 1, 2008

Oklahoma
delay indefinite

Arkansas
Oct 1,
2005

Tennessee

North Carolina

D.C.
Jan 1, 2001

Mississippi

Alabama

Georgia

South
Carolina

Texas
Jan 1, 2002

Louisiana

Florida

Alaska

MEXICO

Hawaii

**Full retail access
for all customers.**

Restructuring active

Restructuring delayed

Restructuring not active

Restructuring suspended

Source: Energy Information Administration.

Many states have at least considered deregulating their electricity businesses.

distinguished economists and supporters of President Franklin Roosevelt's New Deal, always had spoken of free-market economist Milton Friedman with disdain. "He was the devil figure in my youth," Summers said. "Only with time have I come to have large amounts of grudging respect. And, with time, increasingly ungrudging respect."

Deregulation of the Telephone Industry

Many of the regulatory plans of the early part of the century were justified under the theory of "natural monopoly." The telephone system run by AT&T, also known as "Ma Bell" in its heyday, was the prime example. Building telephone lines to every home and business in the country was expensive. If many companies were allowed to compete in building those facilities, they might engage in costly duplication, with little hope of ever recouping their investment.

Instead, industry executives and econo mists argued in unison that AT&T should be seen as a benign and necessary monop oly, should be protected from competition and should be regulated to ensure that i would serve the public interest.

AT&T jealously guarded its monopoly arguing that competition would undercu both service and prices. An upstart entre preneur by the name of William McGowar launched an attack on the phone company in the 1960s, however, starting a firm called Microwave Communications, Inc.— later MCI—to compete with AT&T in pro viding long distance telephone services. In 1974 the Justice Department filed an antitrust suit against AT&T. The court case lasted for nearly a decade and ultimately led to the breakup of AT&T into a long dis tance company (that would have to com pete with the likes of MCI) and multiple regional companies—known as the "baby bells"—to provide local service.

Deregulation of the telephone system took another step forward in 1996, when Congress passed legislation to open phone service to further competition. During the debate over the 1996 law, proponents argued that technology had eliminated the need for regulation. Even if telephone companies had a monopoly on local phone lines, the proponents of deregulation argued, they would face stiff competition in the future from cable companies, wireless companies, and satellite companies. That competition would ensure that Adam Smith's invisible hand did its work, keeping prices down and quality up.

A similar argument was made by the Microsoft Corporation as it battled a U.S. government effort to dismantle its monopoly. Concerns about monopoly were misplaced in the new world of technology, Microsoft's lawyers argued, because the rapid pace of technological innovation ensured that any monopoly would be temporary, soon toppled by new and more powerful technologies.

Electricity Deregulation in the 1990s

In the late 1990s, the electricity industry became the focus of deregulation efforts. A number of states passed laws to allow businesses and consumers to choose from a variety of electricity suppliers, much as they chose among long distance phone carriers. A television advertisement in Pennsylvania captured the moment. It showed a young couple in a romantic apartment in Paris. The man was desperately trying to convince the woman to stay with him and build a new life in the City of Love. The woman appeared willing, except for one troubling detail. Would she be able to choose her electricity supplier? "Whoa," the man said, taken aback. "Where do you think you are, Pennsylvania?"

Like the telephone industry, the electricity business had long been deemed a natural monopoly. Companies had to make large investments up front to build generating plants and install electrical wires. In return, they wanted the government to protect them from competition and guarantee them a healthy profit. So local utility commissions developed a system of cost plus pricing. Utilities were allowed to charge prices to consumers that enabled them to recover all their costs, and then make a reasonable profit on top.

Over time, however, that system encouraged companies to make huge mistakes, and it forced consumers to pay for the mistakes. Utilities that invested in costly nuclear plants in the 1960s and 1970s, for instance, were allowed to charge their customers high rates throughout the 1970s and 1980s, even though the plants sometimes turned out to be unnecessary. Electricity rates varied widely. By the 1990s an electricity user in Pittsburgh was paying rates that were nearly double those paid just 50 miles away in Uniontown, Pennsylvania. Consumers in New York state, which had the most expensive electricity in the nation, were paying on average three times as much as consumers in the state of Washington, which benefited from cheap hydropower generated by government-built dams.

The idea behind deregulation was to open up the electricity system, allowing power consumers in Pittsburgh to buy the same cheap power available in Uniontown. Over time, the theory went, consumers

Portland, Maine, at night. Electricity in Maine was deregulated in 2000.

Airline security personnel load baggage onto an X-ray machine at Boston's Logan Airport in 2002. In the wake of the 2001 terrorist attacks, the U.S government stepped in to federalize airport security.

Meanwhile, state and local governments joined the deregulation trend, turning over more and more public services to private companies. Garbage collection services, public transportation services, welfare offices, prisons, and even police forces were contracted to profit-making companies. Even some public schools were taken over by private companies. The idea was that the power of the marketplace could cure many of the problems created by government bureaucracies.

The steady march toward deregulation, privatization, and reliance on the marketplace contributed to the unprecedented prosperity of the last decade of the twentieth century. As the new century began, however, signs that the trend might have run its course were evident. The terrorist attacks on New York City and Washington, D.C., on September 11, 2001, prompted many to begin rethinking the role of government in the economy. Concerns about security increased and attention to the economic efficiencies that come from private markets correspondingly waned. Congress quickly authorized the federal government to take over the airlines security system, and plans for privatization of government services in many communities were put on hold. National security always had been a constitutionally designated responsibility of the federal government, however, so renewed attention to government programs related to security and defense does not necessarily imply a general reversal of the deregulatory trend.

would get the lowest possible prices, and inefficient power-generating plants would be shut down.

Electricity deregulation ran into trouble in 2000, however, when California's deregulation plan caused a crisis that bankrupted some of the state's utilities and forced residents to suffer rolling brown-outs and black-outs. The California experience was a reminder that deregulation is no panacea—particularly if done in a haphazard or poorly thought-out manner. California had deregulated energy suppliers, requiring utilities to buy electricity from multiple suppliers at variable rates. But the state continued to cap the rates paid by consumers. When supplies got tight, the state's utilities found themselves stuck with ever-higher prices for wholesale energy but unable to cover their costs by raising prices to consumers.

Further Reading

Kahn, Alfred. *Economics of Regulation: Principles and Institutions.* Cambridge, Mass.: MIT Press, 1988.

Murray, Alan. *The Wealth of Choices.* New York: Crown Business, 2000.

Smith, Adam. *The Wealth of Nations.* 1776. Reprint, New York: Modern Library, 1994.

Stigler, George. *Memoirs of an Unregulated Economist.* New York: Basic Books, 1988.

Yergen, Daniel, and Joseph Stanislaw. *The Commanding Heights.* New York: Simon & Schuster, 1998.

—*Alan Murray*

Disposable Income

Most people are fascinated by income and consumption. Expensive cars and homes are interpreted as signs of high status and professional success. However, they represent much more: They also reflect the optimism of consumers and allow economists to predict future economic performance. Strong spending on luxuries indicates that consumers feel confident that they can easily afford their basic needs.

Disposable income is defined as the total amount of income received after paying taxes. This money can be either spent or saved for future use. Studies show that the average American spends about 90 percent of his or her income and saves the rest. The portion that households spend is called consumption. This includes spending on basic needs like food, clothing, and shelter, as well as luxuries. Consumption, consisting of roughly two-thirds of all economic activity, is critical to the U.S. economy and totaled roughly $16 trillion in 2000.

Savings is defined as people giving up current consumption to receive additional consumption in the future. This is money that is invested in stocks, placed in bank accounts, and so on with the intention of generating income that can be spent later. Savings is also important in an economy. It provides a pool of money available for entrepreneurs to invest in the creation of new goods and services. This encourages

See also:
Economic Growth; Fiscal Policy; Great Depression; Keynes, John Maynard.

Disposable Income and Personal Expenditures 1959 to 2000

Year	Disposable personal income (in billions of dollars)	Personal consumption expenditures (in billions of dollars)	Population (in thousands)	Year	Disposable personal income (in billions of dollars)	Personal consumption expenditures (in billions of dollars)	Population (in thousands)
1959	1,624	1,471	177,130	1980	3,658	3,193	227,726
1960	1,665	1,511	180,760	1981	3,741	3,236	230,008
1961	1,720	1,541	183,742	1982	3,792	3,276	232,218
1962	1,804	1,617	186,590	1983	3,907	3,454	234,332
1963	1,872	1,684	189,300	1984	4,208	3,641	236,394
1964	2,007	1,785	191,927	1985	4,348	3,821	238,506
1965	2,131	1,898	194,347	1986	4,487	3,981	240,682
1966	2,245	2,006	196,599	1987	4,583	4,113	242,842
1967	2,340	2,066	198,752	1988	4,784	4,280	245,061
1968	2,448	2,184	200,745	1989	4,907	4,394	247,387
1969	2,524	2,265	202,736	1990	5,014	4,475	249,981
1970	2,630	2,318	205,089	1991	5,033	4,467	253,336
1971	2,745	2,405	207,692	1992	5,189	4,595	256,677
1972	2,874	2,551	209,924	1993	5,261	4,749	260,037
1973	3,072	2,676	211,939	1994	5,397	4,928	263,226
1974	3,052	2,654	213,898	1995	5,539	5,076	266,364
1975	3,109	2,711	215,981	1996	5,678	5,238	269,485
1976	3,244	2,869	218,086	1997	5,855	5,424	272,756
1977	3,361	2,992	220,289	1998	6,169	5,684	275,955
1978	3,528	3,125	222,629	1999	6,320	5,968	279,144
1979	3,629	3,203	225,106	2000	6,539	6,258	282,489

Note: In constant 1996 dollars.
Source: Economic Report to the President, 2002.

The projected impact on the economy as a whole of a change in consumption of $1 billion is given in this table. The marginal propensity to consume is the portion of each dollar of disposable income that is consumed rather than saved. The money multiplier is a mathematical calculation that enables economists to estimate the broader impact of a change in consumption.

Consumption and Output

Marginal Propensity to Consume (MPC)	Money Multiplier	Economic Impact*
.95	20	$20 billion
.90	10	$10 billion
.75	4	$4 billion
.50	2	$2 billion

*Based on a consumption change of $1 billion.
Source: Economic Report to the President, 2002.

K-Mart's huge store near Pennsylvania Station in New York City is targeted at commuters. In the eyes of many economists, the more people are willing to spend, the healthier the economy.

the creation of new goods and services that can make society better off.

The table on page 363 shows the relationships between disposable income, savings, and consumer spending. It shows that total disposable income in the United States has increased since 1960, from roughly $1.6 trillion to $6.5 trillion in 2000.

This increase is attributable, in part, to the more than 50 percent increase in the population during this period. However, the overall increase is far greater than the increase in population. The rest of the increase is a result of economic growth.

Total economic production, measured by gross domestic product, roughly tripled in this period, resulting in rising incomes.

The table also shows a relatively constant relationship between disposable income and consumer spending. In short, money that is earned but not spent is defined as savings, which has averaged about 10 percent of disposable income for the past 40 years. The relationship between income and savings is called the consumption function, which plays a central role in the development of economic theory in the twentieth century.

In October 1929 the U.S. stock market collapsed and the world plunged into the Great Depression, which lasted for more than 10 years and caused high unemployment, poverty, and other problems around the world. The conventional economic wisdom that business downturns would correct themselves was clearly inadequate to explain why the Depression lasted so long.

John Maynard Keynes, who later won the Nobel prize for economics, provided an explanation for the depth and severity of the Great Depression. He created the Keynesian model, which predicted economic output based on consumption, government spending, and other variables. One of Keynes's most important insights was that consumption expenditures, by either individual households or by the entire population, are heavily influenced by income. During depressions, unemployment rises and incomes drop, with a resulting reduction in consumption and overall economic output.

Keynes's model has two mechanisms. The first is called the marginal propensity to consume (MPC). It represents the fraction of each dollar of disposable income that is consumed, and is typically around 0.9. Thus, for each increase or decrease of income by $1, consumption either rises or falls by 90 cents.

The second mechanism is called the money multiplier. Using extensive mathematical proofs, Keynes showed that a change in consumption or government spending has a ripple effect through an economy. Thus, if the

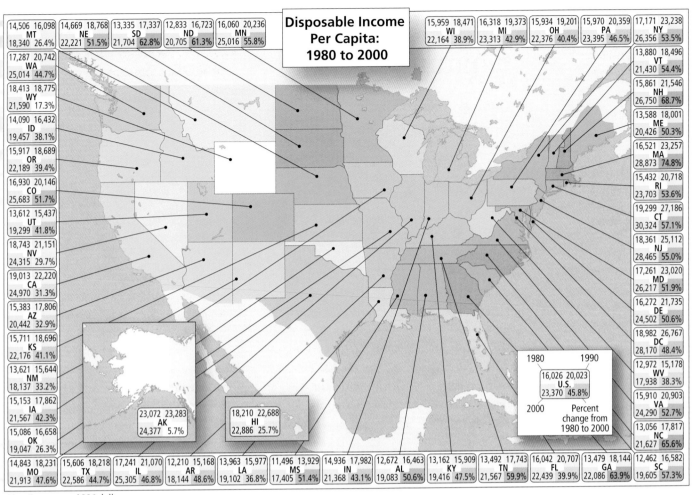

Disposable Income Per Capita: 1980 to 2000

	1980	1990
	14,506	16,098
MT	18,340	26.4%

	1980	1990
	14,669	18,768
NE	22,221	51.5%

	1980	1990
	13,335	17,337
SD	21,704	62.8%

	1980	1990
	12,833	16,723
ND	20,705	61.3%

	1980	1990
	16,060	20,236
MN	25,016	55.8%

	1980	1990
	15,959	18,471
WI	22,164	38.9%

	1980	1990
	16,318	19,373
MI	23,313	42.9%

	1980	1990
	15,934	19,201
OH	22,376	40.4%

	1980	1990
	15,970	20,359
PA	23,395	46.5%

	1980	1990
	17,171	23,238
NY	26,356	53.5%

	1980	1990
	17,287	20,742
WA	25,014	44.7%

	1980	1990
	13,880	18,496
VT	21,430	54.4%

	1980	1990
	18,413	18,775
WY	21,590	17.3%

	1980	1990
	15,861	21,546
NH	26,750	68.7%

	1980	1990
	14,090	16,432
ID	19,457	38.1%

	1980	1990
	13,588	18,001
ME	20,426	50.3%

	1980	1990
	15,917	18,689
OR	22,189	39.4%

	1980	1990
	16,521	23,257
MA	28,873	74.8%

	1980	1990
	16,930	20,146
CO	25,683	51.7%

	1980	1990
	15,432	20,718
RI	23,703	53.6%

	1980	1990
	13,612	15,437
UT	19,299	41.8%

	1980	1990
	19,299	27,186
CT	30,324	57.1%

	1980	1990
	18,743	21,151
NV	24,315	29.7%

	1980	1990
	18,361	25,112
NJ	28,465	55.0%

	1980	1990
	19,013	22,220
CA	24,970	31.3%

	1980	1990
	17,261	23,020
MD	26,217	51.9%

	1980	1990
	15,383	17,806
AZ	20,442	32.9%

	1980	1990
	16,272	21,735
DE	24,502	50.6%

	1980	1990
	15,711	18,696
KS	22,176	41.1%

	1980	1990
	18,982	26,767
DC	28,170	48.4%

	1980	1990
	13,621	15,644
NM	18,137	33.2%

	1980	1990
	12,972	15,178
WV	17,938	38.3%

	1980	1990
	15,153	17,862
IA	21,567	42.3%

	1980	1990
	15,910	20,903
VA	24,290	52.7%

	1980	1990
	15,086	16,658
OK	19,047	26.3%

	1980	1990
	13,056	17,817
NC	21,627	65.6%

AK: 23,072 / 23,283 / 24,377 / 5.7%

HI: 18,210 / 22,688 / 22,886 / 25.7%

	1980	1990
	16,026	20,023
U.S.	23,370	45.8%

2000 — Percent change from 1980 to 2000

	1980	1990
	14,843	18,231
MO	21,913	47.6%

	1980	1990
	15,606	18,218
TX	22,586	44.7%

	1980	1990
	17,241	21,070
IL	25,305	46.8%

	1980	1990
	12,210	15,168
AR	18,144	48.6%

	1980	1990
	13,963	15,977
LA	19,102	36.8%

	1980	1990
	11,496	13,929
MS	17,405	51.4%

	1980	1990
	14,936	17,982
IN	21,368	43.1%

	1980	1990
	12,672	16,463
AL	19,083	50.6%

	1980	1990
	13,162	15,909
KY	19,416	47.5%

	1980	1990
	13,492	17,743
TN	21,567	59.9%

	1980	1990
	16,042	20,707
FL	22,439	39.9%

	1980	1990
	13,479	18,144
GA	22,086	63.9%

	1980	1990
	12,462	16,582
SC	19,605	57.3%

Note: In constant 1996 dollars.

Source: U.S. Bureau of Economic Analysis. *Survey of Current Business.* Washington, D.C., 2001.

MPC is 0.9 and consumption drops by $1 billion because of recession, the result will be a $10 billion decrease in overall economic output. The opposite also holds true: if consumption increases by $1 billion, total economic output will subsequently rise by $10 billion. (See chart on page 365.)

Keynes used this logic to argue that the Great Depression could be cured. He explained that consumers were either unable or unwilling to spend. Therefore, the solution was a massive increase in government spending to provide jobs. This investment in jobs would result in increased disposable incomes, leading to more consumption, which would revive the economy. The administration of President Franklin Roosevelt agreed and began an unprecedented increase in government spending.

The experience of the Great Depression led to the creation of national fiscal policy, the process of managing economic booms and busts by adjusting government spending to stabilize incomes and economic performance. Part of Keynes's legacy is that disposable income still plays a central role in understanding the economy and in national economic policy.

Disposable income also still plays a central role in economic theory. It indicates current consumer wealth, optimism, and willingness to spend. These data can be analyzed to predict the need for and likely impact of government economic policies.

Further Reading

Galbraith, John Kenneth. *The Affluent Society.* 1958. Reprint, New York: Houghton Mifflin, 1998.

Mansfield, Edwin, and Nariman Behravesh. *Economics USA.* 5th ed. New York: W. W. Norton, 1998.

—*David Long*

Distribution Channels

Distribution channels, or marketing channels as they are also known, direct the flow of goods from producers to final customers. Direct channels, in which the producer sells to the customer without the assistance of third parties, exist in both consumer and business markets. More often, however, distribution channels include market intermediaries or middlemen like wholesalers, retailers, brokers, manufacturers' agents, or industrial distributors.

Members of distribution channels perform critical tasks for the final customer. They make products available at the times and places consumers or business buyers demand them, and they permit those customers to obtain ownership of goods or to use them through rental or leasing agreements. Market intermediaries also provide important assistance to their channel partners. They gather market information, facilitate customer relationships, develop product assortments, coordinate promotional activities, establish pricing policies, aid in financing inventories, and manage the physical distribution of goods.

Because marketing intermediaries must be paid for the services they perform, their presence in the distribution channel does raise the final price of goods paid by customers. Critics have argued that this price increase, also known as the middleman's markup, is excessive, and perhaps even parasitic. Supporters, however, counter that channel members make marketing exchanges efficient by eliminating the need for every producer to interact with every customer. For example, if four consumers wish to examine four brands of cereal, a total of 16 producer–customer contacts are necessary. By placing the four cereal brands with an intermediary like a retail store, the number of interactions is reduced to eight.

Moreover, channel members perform essential services that must occur with or without intermediaries. Because middlemen often are focused on providing particular marketing functions, the channel and its final customers may benefit from the improved performance resulting from specialization and from cost reductions associated with economies of scale.

Kinds of Channels

Distribution channels are present in both the consumer and business marketplaces.

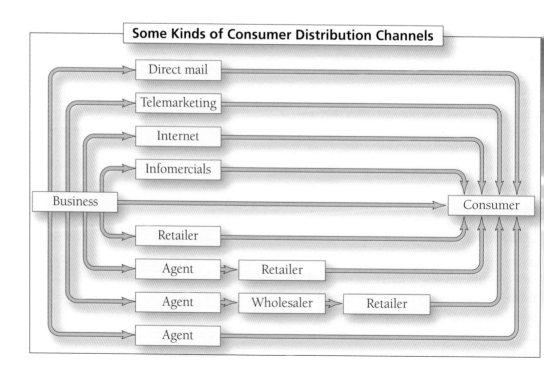

Some Kinds of Consumer Distribution Channels

Distribution Intensity		
Intensive Distribution • Many outlets • Multiple distribution channels *Examples* soft drinks; newspapers; cleaning supplies	**Selective Distribution** • Limited number of outlets • Outlets screened to provide appropriate services *Examples* major appliances; business equipment	**Exclusive Distribution** • One outlet in large geographic area • Channel members carry full product line, employ highly trained sales people; provide superior customer service • Retailer is only intermediary in distribution chain *Examples* expensive consumer specialty goods; major industrial equipment

The number of intermediaries in both kinds of channels depends upon the nature of the product being distributed. Another factor involved in shaping the structure of distribution channels is the firm's need to satisfy consumer demand regarding what products and services are available and at which points they are available.

Producers, who wish to reach consumers, have a number of options. Through catalogs, mailing pieces, television infomercials, telemarketing, and the Internet, they may sell directly to their customers. Alternatively, producers may sell to large retailers, who, in turn, make the product available to consumers. A third kind of channel extends from producers to wholesalers to large numbers of smaller retailers and ultimately to consumers. Finally, to achieve mass distribution of a product in a variety of outlets, the producer can use the lengthiest channel whereby the product reaches the consumer after passing through the hands of agents or brokers, wholesalers, and retailers.

Like their consumer goods counterparts, producers of products designed for business customers may consider a variety of channel arrangements. They may use a specially trained sales force, catalogs, or the Internet to sell directly to their customers. Such direct channels account for more than half of the sales of all business products. Producers of business products also use marketing intermediaries. Those that sell goods of low or moderate value frequently sell their output to industrial distributors, who hold inventories and resell in small quantities to users. Those that require sales support for their products may use the services of manufacturers' agents, who represent the complementary products of several noncompeting firms in a given territory. Last, producers who wish to do business in a large geographic area but lack a sales force may reach their customers through a channel composed of agents and industrial distributors.

The selection of one distribution channel does not preclude the use of others. Producers of goods destined for both consumer and business customers generally employ separate channels to reach their respective markets. Producers may also target consumers or business segments with distinct distribution requirements or preferences. As a consequence, they may use a direct channel to serve some customers, but make goods available through a retail outlet, an industrial distributor, or combination of channel members to meet the needs of others. The use of multiple distribution channels, known as dual distribution, is a common practice, but the perception that one channel may be benefiting at the expense of another is a frequent cause of channel conflict.

Producers who distribute products outside the United States must often accommodate different channel structures that exist abroad. In Japan, for example, consumer goods channels generally include three wholesale levels—national or primary wholesalers, secondary or regional wholesalers, and local wholesalers—that in combination serve large numbers of extremely small retailers. When considering foreign distribution channels, businesses also need to take into account the consumer cultures and the existing technological and transportation infrastructures in the nations where they plan to do business. Such considerations are important because they may dictate the kinds of outlets in which goods need to be available or because they limit the possibilities of reaching customers through, for example, catalogs or Internet Web sites.

Distribution Intensity

Choices relating to channel structure are closely related to distribution intensity, or the degree to which a product is available to its customers. Market coverage is generally classified into three categories: intensive, selective, or exclusive. The nature of the product being handled together with the purchase behaviors of intended consumers or business buyers guide availability decisions.

Intensive distribution, which places a product in as many outlets as possible, is appropriate for convenience goods.

Consumers frequently replenish items like soft drinks, bread, and newspapers, and expect them to be readily available. Likewise, business buyers want easy access to such goods as copy paper or cleaning supplies. Given the need to maximize market coverage, producers of such products generally rely on multiple distribution channels and include those with several levels of middlemen to assure product availability not only in major outlets but also in vending machines and at small retail shops and industrial distributors.

Selective distribution places products in a limited number of outlets that are chosen using criteria like ability to provide sales support, warranty service, or an appropriate selling atmosphere. Selective distribution is common for most shopping goods and some specialty goods, including major appliances or business accessory equipment. Consumers and business customers give thought and effort when purchasing these higher-priced goods, and they will forgo the convenience of easy availability to obtain better product information or other services at the point of sale. Channels for selectively distributed products tend to have fewer levels of intermediaries than do channels for convenience goods.

Exclusive distribution allows only one outlet in a relatively large geographic area to distribute a product. Expensive consumer specialty goods and major industrial equipment are typical of the kinds of products with highly restricted availability. In return for exclusive rights, channel members generally carry a full product line, employ highly trained salespeople, and provide superior customer service. Retailers and distributors with exclusive rights are commonly the only intermediaries in the distribution channel.

Channel Cooperation

Distribution channels are composed of independent firms that must depend upon one another to achieve the common goal of making goods available to the customer. This goal necessitates a high level of cooperation in a distribution channel, and, at

The vertical marketing system can be more efficient than a conventional marketing channel because the vertical channel imposes uniform processes.

Conventional Marketing Channel vs. Vertical Marketing System

Conventional Marketing Channel	Vertical Marketing System
Manufacturer	Manufacturer Wholesaler Retailer
Wholesaler	
Retailer	
Consumer	Consumer

The enormous success of Wal-Mart is partly attributable to the company's firm and efficient control of its vertical marketing system.

the same time, suggests the possibility for conflict among channel members. Clear and timely communication among the members of the distribution channel, which has been facilitated by the Internet, is the best means of avoiding frustration and facilitating the smooth operation of partner relationships.

Some channels rely upon a channel captain to provide leadership and to organize member responsibilities. The captain may come from any level of the distribution channel but must have the authority to influence the performance of the other channel partners. Examples of captains of their respective channels include the major automobile manufacturers; the retail giant, Wal-Mart; and the grocery wholesaler, the Independent Grocers' Alliance.

One structure for distribution channels is the vertical marketing system (VMS), in which all aspects of the chain from producer to final seller are unified. A VMS offers an important means of assuring that channel activities are appropriately performed. The

contractual VMS is the most common type of vertical marketing system.

In a contractual VMS, legal agreements, enforceable in court, identify the rights and responsibilities of respective channel members. Franchises are contractual VMSs.

In an administered VMS, channel members remain independent, but informal coordination is facilitated by the adoption of common inventory systems, accounting procedures, or other uniform processes. A channel captain generally plays a leadership role in an administered system.

The corporate VMS makes possible the highest level of channel control. In such systems, all channel members have a common corporate owner.

Further Reading

Coughlan, Anne T., Erin Anderson, et al. *Marketing Channels.* 6th ed. Upper Saddle River, N.J.: Prentice-Hall, 2001.

The Stanford Global Supply Chain Management Forum, http://corporate.stanford.edu/research/programs/supchn.html (January 6, 2003).

—*Marilyn Lavin*

Division of Labor

Division of labor is splitting a job or a task between two or more people. Although the idea is a simple one, its consequences are enormous, including the transformation of work, the Industrial Revolution, and a general increase in the goods and services available to all members of society.

People have always worked to satisfy their needs and wants. Before the Industrial Revolution most people in the world lived in small villages with limited technology and trade. This required self-sufficiency, so people spent much of their time doing basic tasks, including growing food and making their own cloth. Progress and invention were minimal because of limited education and the general lack of tools.

The effects of the division of labour, in the general business of society, will be more easily understood by considering in what manner it operates in some particular manufactures. . . . To take an example, therefore, from a very trifling manufacture; but one in which the division of labour has been very often taken notice of, the trade of the pin-maker; a workman not educated to this business (which the division of labour has rendered a distinct trade), nor acquainted with the use of the machinery employed in it (to the invention of which the same division of labour has probably given occasion), could scarce, perhaps, with his utmost industry, make one pin in a day, and certainly could not make twenty. But in the way in which this business is now carried on, not only the whole work is a peculiar trade, but it is divided into a number of branches, of which the greater part are likewise peculiar trades. One man draws out the wire, another straights it, a third cuts it, a fourth points it, a fifth grinds it at the top for receiving the head; to make the head requires two or three distinct operations; to put it on is a peculiar business, to whiten the pins is another; it is even a trade by itself to put them into the paper; and the important business of making a pin is, in this manner, divided into about eighteen distinct operations. . . .

I have seen a small manufactory of this kind where ten men only were employed, and where some of them consequently performed two or three distinct operations. But though they were very poor, and therefore but indifferently accommodated with the necessary machinery, they could, when they exerted themselves, make among them about twelve pounds of pins in a day. There are in a pound upwards of four thousand pins of a middling size. Those ten persons, therefore, could make among them upwards of forty-eight thousand pins in a day. Each person, therefore, making a tenth part of forty-eight thousand pins, might be considered as making four thousand eight hundred pins in a day. But if they had all wrought separately and independently, and without any of them having been educated to this peculiar business, they certainly could not each of them have made twenty, perhaps not one pin in a day; that is, certainly, not the two hundred and fortieth, perhaps not the four thousand eight hundredth part of what they are at present capable of performing, in consequence of a proper division and combination of their different operations.

—Adam Smith, *The Wealth of Nations*, 1776

More complicated tasks were called crafts or skilled trades, and included carpentry, smithing, and so on. These jobs required years of training, special tools, and materials. As these were scarce, few people in society could become craftsmen.

Craftsmen had a great economic advantage because they had a monopoly on their specialty and could charge premium prices for the services and goods they produced. In Europe during the Middle Ages they increased this advantage by forming guilds, or unions, for each craft. All of the tradesmen in a craft agreed on set prices and limited entry into the trade, keeping production low, prices high, and enriching the guildsmen.

Limited technology encouraged this system. Most items had to be produced one at a time as few machines had been invented and energy sources were limited. Tradesmen used craft production, meaning they either did all of the work by hand or directed apprentices through the process. Finished work could be of great beauty and quality, but the quantity was always limited.

Starting in England around 1750, the Industrial Revolution brought about great change. Plentiful energy sources—coal, wind, and water power—were mastered, which enabled managers to employ more complex machinery and technology. Entrepreneurs invented machines to do the work and built large factories to replace the smaller workshops of craftsmen. Unlike master craftsmen, factory workers required little education to tend the machines and could produce enormous amounts of goods. Mass production had arrived.

Adam Smith was the first economist to notice the tremendous possibilities of redesigning work. In his masterpiece, *The Wealth of Nations* (1776), he used a pin factory as an example. One worker alone would produce fewer than 20 pins in a day. However, by dividing the tasks into smaller steps and using machines for mass production, many thousands of pins could be produced. This is the heart of the concept of division of labor: subdividing the tasks

required to produce a good increases the ability of the factory to increase production.

Over time, entrepreneurs redesigned the workplace for mass production. Factory work became dominated by the assembly line, where each step in the production process was done in order from start to finish. Each worker had one small, specific task that he or she repeated for each item, and overall output increased dramatically.

One negative effect was the new nature of work. Employment in the new urban factories was dreary at best. Work was now specialized into small tasks, and factory workers soon became bored. Moreover, the factories were crowded, loud, and unsafe. Employers demanded long hours and permitted harsh working conditions to maximize their profits, often employing women and children because their smaller hands were better able to operate the machines.

The social consequences of changing from craft to mass production were tremendous. Cities grew rapidly during the 1800s as people moved from the countryside to work in the factories. Poorly paid workers usually lived in crowded substandard housing with little medical care or education. These conditions, combined with the growing populations of unsatisfied workers, led to political changes in the late nineteenth and early twentieth centuries. Workers organized unions to represent their interests, and politicians slowly became more responsive to the demands of workers

An undated engraving of an early Westinghouse assembly line, circa nineteenth century.

Production through History

Middle Ages
Trade Production:
Tradesman does all work by hand or by directing apprentices

Industrial Revolution
Mass Production:
Each worker repeats one, small specific task

Twenty-First Century
Flexible Specialization:
Teams use technology to perform different tasks

The concept of division of labor has been transferred to management structures; different managers are assigned responsibility for various aspects of a project.

for better wages and working conditions. At the same time, American business leaders took the idea of division of labor beyond the factory floor and into the boardroom. Management structures evolved to, in effect, divide the labor of managing a large workforce.

Overall, the economic results of the Industrial Revolution were dramatically positive. Using the new machines, workers could produce far more, bringing prices down for consumers, who also gained from having a greater variety of goods to purchase. Factory owners benefited because profits rose; they could make more money by selling more goods at a lower price. Some of the new profits were reinvested in the business and resulted in further improvements in productivity.

This combination of economic and social changes allowed the workers to demand higher wages. Over time, using unions, strikes, and political pressure, workers were able to gain pay increases and see their standard of living slowly rise. In time, many factory workers became middle class, especially in America, and poverty rates declined dramatically.

The late twentieth century saw further advances in the assembly line system. Competition forces businesses to constantly find new and better ways to operate. Seeking to increase profits and quality while reducing production time, companies have reorganized work to use computers and more sophisticated machines. Such changes resulted in a new model of production called flexible specialization, which is a combination of craft and mass production. The process is flexible because the workers are trained to use technology to perform different tasks. They also work in teams to solve problems and develop better methods of production. As a consequence, businesses can better produce a variety of quality goods in large quantities, serving the needs of a broad range of customers and thus increasing earnings.

One result is that manufacturing work is now more challenging and varied. Work-teams are responsible both for completing multiple portions of the assembly process and for finding more efficient ways to perform their assignments. Another result is that companies want workers with a much broader range of skills than in the past. Unlike the assembly line, flexible specialization requires employees with the ability to solve problems, work with technology, and operate effectively in teams.

Further Reading

Chandler, Alfred D. *The Visible Hand: The Managerial Revolution in American Business.* Cambridge, Mass.: Belknap Press, 1977.

Heilbroner, Robert, and William Milberg. *The Making of Economic Society.* 11th ed. Upper Saddle River, N.J.: Prentice Hall, 2002.

—*David Long*

Dow Chemical Company

Dow has pioneered advances in chemical engineering, organic chemistry, and metallurgy. Some of the company's products have been denounced for their use in warfare and for their effects on human health and the environment. As the largest chemical company in the United States, and the maker of a wide variety of products that include Prozac, Styrofoam, napalm, Agent Orange, and silicone breast implants, Dow Chemical is almost as infamous as it is famous.

Dow Chemical Company was founded by Herbert Henry Dow (1866–1930), a professor of chemical engineering who had developed a very efficient process for extracting bromine, chlorine, and other chemicals from brine (a salt and mineral-rich liquid found in ancient, underground seas). Many of the company's early products were based on a class of chemicals called halogens (group VII on the periodic table), which include bromine, chlorine, iodine, and fluorine.

Dow founded the Midland Chemical Company in 1890 to extract bromine from brine. Midland, Ohio, was chosen because of the large quantities of brine in the area. Although successful, Dow fell out with his financial backers when he wanted to diversify. Dow left Midland and formed the Dow Process Company, which used electrolysis to make bleach. Dow Process then merged with Midland in 1897 to form the Dow Chemical Company.

Dow could produce bromine cheaply, but the company was threatened by the German bromine cartel, which set the prices for all bromine sold outside the United States. The cartel flooded the American market with below-cost bromine in an attempt to destroy the company. Dow responded by stopping its manufacture of bromine, purchasing the below-market-cost imported bromine, then repackaging it and reselling it in Europe and Japan below the German cartel's normal prices. By the time the cartel realized what had happened, Dow controlled world bromine prices. Later, Dow would use a similar strategy to break the German magnesium cartel.

With the market secured, Dow Chemical began diversifying, first into chlorine chemicals, then organic chemicals like phenol and indigo dye, and then into magnesium, metal, and plastics. Dow was also the largest producer in the world of common items like Epsom salts. During Herbert Dow's lifetime the company obtained its bromine, chlorine, sodium, calcium, and magnesium from the brine of ancient seas under Midland, but Dow Chemical later developed experimental processes to mine the minerals from the oceans.

Many of Dow's products were developed for use by the military. During World War I, Dow produced chemicals used to

See also:
Agriculture Industry; Defense Industry; Environmental Protection Agency.

Dow Chemical Company

1890
Herbert Henry Dow founds the Midland Chemical Company.

1897
Dow Chemical Company formed from a merger of Dow Process and Midland.

1914–1918
Dow produces chemicals for use in World War I.

1933
Ralph Wiley discovers eonite, which becomes Saran Wrap.

1962–1971
The herbicide Agent Orange used in the Vietnam War.

1984
Dow settles lawsuit with Vietnam War veterans and their families.

1999
Dow merges with Union Carbide.

make explosives, medicines, flares, tear gas, and mustard gas. The company was also the first to manufacture synthetic indigo, used as a dye. After the war, Dow developed a method for using magnesium left over from explosives production to make lightweight engine parts for cars and airplanes and a bromine-based fuel additive to prevent engine knocking.

Many of the plastics we use today for everything from toys to car parts were first invented or manufactured at Dow. Company laboratories invented plastics, among them polystyrene, polyurethane, polypropylene, and latex, and created a number of common household products—Ziploc Bags, Fantastik Cleaner, Handi-Wrap, Spray 'N Wash, Ultra Yes laundry detergent, Vivid bleach, and Style and Perma Soft hair products.

In 1933, Ralph Wiley, a college student who cleaned glassware in a Dow Chemical lab, came across a vial he could not scrub clean. He called the substance eonite, after an

indestructible material in the popular comic strip "Little Orphan Annie." He mentioned the sticky chemical to researchers in the lab, who developed the goop, polyvinylidene chloride, into a dark green protective film, then into the product Saran Wrap.

Since its founding, Dow has formed more than 30 subsidiaries to conduct research and manufacture products in different areas. In the 1930s, Dow Chemical formed the subsidiary Ethyl Dow Company to extract bromine for use in antiknock engines. Ten years later, Dow Chemical and Corning Glass merged to form Dow Corning, which produces silicones for the military and other uses; Dow Corning declared bankruptcy in 1995, largely brought about by the numerous lawsuits involving silicone breast implants made by the company. DowElanco (formed with the pharmaceutical company Eli Lilly) is the largest producer of pesticides and fungicides in the United States The company joined with DuPont to form DuPont Dow Elastomers. In 1999, Dow merged with Union Carbide despite concerns about Union Carbide's continuing financial liability from the Bhopal disaster (a 1984 accident at Union Carbide's plant in Bhopal, India, that killed thousands of people).

Some of the company's products that were first developed for military use include lightweight metals and silicones for use in airplanes and spacecraft (the heat shield on Apollo 8 was made with Dow epoxy resin) and chemical defoliants and weapons materials. During the Vietnam War, Dow was targeted by antiwar activists because of its production of napalm, an incendiary product. Dow was also one of the makers of Agent Orange, an herbicide made from the chlorine-based chemical dioxin; Agent Orange was used in fighting the Vietnam War and is now believed to be responsible for severe health problems for both American veterans and Vietnamese survivors. In a 1984 out-of-court settlement with veterans and their families, Dow joined other chemical companies in creating a $180 million fund for American military personnel exposed to Agent Orange.

A student going for an interview (right) is assisted by an official (left) as he climbs over a sea of protesters outside the recruiting office of Dow Chemical at the State University of New York at Albany. The protesters targeted Dow because of its production of napalm, an incendiary material used frequently during the Vietnam War.

A toxicology lab at Dow Chemical, in Midland, Ohio.

Dow is said to rank sixth in the world in production of toxic chemical waste, carcinogens, and ozone-depleting chemicals. The company has also come under a great deal of scrutiny for selling chemical pesticides overseas that have been banned in the United States because of their effects on health. Nevertheless, *Fortune* magazine named Dow one of America's "Top 10 Environmental Champions," and the company has had strict world pollution control guidelines in place since 1971. Company shareholders and environmentalists have raised questions about the company's involvement in the development of genetically modified crops. Many of these crops are engineered to be resistant to particular pesticides—pesticides also manufactured by Dow.

Controversy is perhaps inevitable for a company that makes many chemicals that,

while being incredibly useful, are also toxic. Nevertheless, Dow is a leader in science and technology, with annual sales in the neighborhood of $30 billion and customers in more than 170 countries. Several times every day, most Americans use a product made by Dow.

Further Reading

Bowden, Mary Ellen. *Chemical Achievers.* Philadelphia: Chemical Heritage Foundation, 1997.

Bowden, Mary Ellen, and John Kenly Smith. *American Chemical Enterprise.* Philadelphia: Chemical Heritage Foundation, 1994.

Brandt, E. N. *Growth Company: Dow Chemical's First Century.* East Lansing: Michigan State University Press, 1997.

Whitehead, Don. *The Dow Story: The History of the Dow Chemical Company.* New York: McGraw-Hill, 1968.

—Lisa Magloff

Dow Jones Averages

"How did the market do today?" In response to that question many people reply with either, "The Dow was up" or "The Dow was down." This response refers to the Dow Jones Industrial Average (DJIA), the oldest continuous indicator of the U.S. stock market. The DJIA is, in fact, one of three Dow Jones averages: The others are the Dow Jones Transportation Average (DJTA) and the Dow Jones Utility Average (DJUA).

In 1884, stocks were considered to be risky investments, and investors had difficulty understanding the daily changes in stock prices. Charles Henry Dow attempted to make sense of stock prices by creating an average that tracked the prices of 11 stocks, most of them railroads. As time passed, Dow envisioned an industrial average as a tool that the general public could use to measure the overall performance of the U.S. stock market.

On May 26, 1896, the vision became reality when the DJIA made its debut. The original average began at a level of 40.94 and consisted of the leading industrial companies of the time, including General Electric, American Tobacco, and U.S. Rubber. In 1902 the editors of the *Wall Street Journal* assumed management of the DJIA. By 1928 the number of stocks in the DJIA had increased to 30.

Changes have been made to the DJIA many of them because of mergers, but some substitutions have been made to maintain the consistency of the DJIA in relation to the broad market. As the economy has become less oriented to manufacturing and more oriented to service and technology, the Dow components have changed accordingly. General Electric is the only company that has remained a part of the DJIA from 1896 to the present.

A significant change in the DJIA occurred on November 1, 1999, when Union Carbide, Goodyear, Chevron, and Sears were replaced with Microsoft, Intel, SBC Communications, and Home Depot. This change was notable also because formerly, all DJIA stocks were traded on the New York Stock Exchange (NYSE). Microsoft and Intel, which trade on the Nasdaq market, became the first DJIA stocks that do not trade on the NYSE.

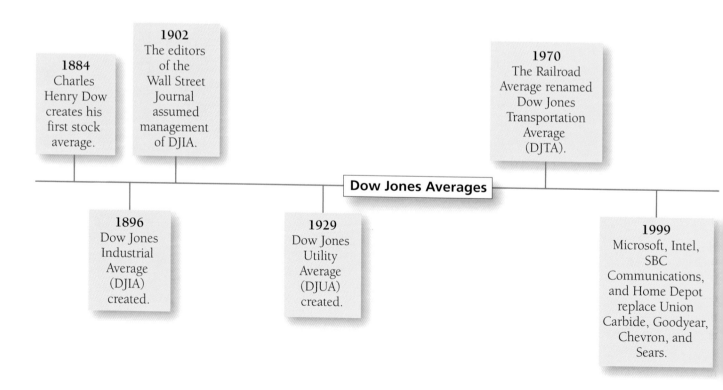

1884
Charles Henry Dow creates his first stock average.

1902
The editors of the Wall Street Journal assumed management of DJIA.

1970
The Railroad Average renamed Dow Jones Transportation Average (DJTA).

Dow Jones Averages

1896
Dow Jones Industrial Average (DJIA) created.

1929
Dow Jones Utility Average (DJUA) created.

1999
Microsoft, Intel, SBC Communications, and Home Depot replace Union Carbide, Goodyear, Chevron, and Sears.

In October 1896, a few months after the debut of the DJIA, Dow's original 11-stock index that was started in 1884 shed the last of its nonrailroad components and became known as the Railroad Average. Throughout the twentieth century, the Railroad Average was expanded to include trucking, airline, and package delivery firms. In 1970, the Railroad Average became the Dow Jones Transportation Average (DJTA). The Transportation Average includes Northwest Air-lines, Federal Express, and U.S. Freight-ways. Union Pacific is the only original stock that remains part of the DJTA.

The Dow Jones Utility Average (DJUA) is the youngest of the three Dow Jones averages, having made its debut in January 1929. The original Utility Average comprised 18 firms; it was increased to 20 firms later in 1929 before being reduced to its current 15 firms in 1938. The Utility Average currently includes large electricity and gas utility companies like Consolidated Edison, PG&E Corporation, and Texas Utilities Company. The original Utility Average included AT&T, which was moved to the DJIA in 1939.

The price-weighted computation method used to determine the Dow Jones Industrial, Transportation, and Utility Averages is unique. Most indexes are market-value weighted. Even though price-weighting introduces a bias because high-priced stocks affect the average more than low-priced stocks, price-weighting was selected when the DJIA was started in 1896 for ease of computation. In 1928 the *Wall Street Journal* began computing the value of the indexes using special divisors instead of the number of stocks in the average. This was done to avoid problems when companies split their shares or substitutions were made in the index. In 2002 the divisor for the DJIA was less than 0.15; therefore, a $1 change in the price of a component stock produced almost a seven-point change in the value of the index.

The Dow Jones Company maintains more than 3,000 indexes that track world

markets. In addition to the DJIA, the company has developed many domestic and international indexes in response to growing demand from the investment community. These innovations include the Dow Jones STOXX Indexes, a group of regional European equity indexes, and the Dow Jones Sector Titans Indexes, a comprehensive family of indexes that track market leaders in sectors such as energy, healthcare, and banking.

Charles Dow (left) and Edward T. Jones

Further Reading

Dow Jones and Co., Inc. Staff. *Dow Jones Guide to the Global Stock Market.* 1999 ed. New York: Dow Jones & Company, 1999.

Dow Jones Indexes, http://www.djindexes.com (January 6, 2003).

Hamilton, William Peter. *The Stock Market Barometer.* 1926. Reprint, New York: John Wiley & Sons, 1998.

Prestbo, John A., ed. *Markets Measure: An Illustrated History of America Told through the Dow Jones Industrial Average.* New York: Dow Jones & Company, 1999.

Raghavan, Anita, and Nancy Ann Jeffrey. "What, How, Why: So What Is the Dow Jones Industrial Average, Anyway?" *The Wall Street Journal,* 28 May 1996.

—*Angeline Lavin*

Downsizing

Business conditions in the late twentieth century led many corporations to make drastic adjustments in their operations. Throughout the 1980s and into the 1990s, many trends, including competition from imports and the adoption of new technologies that rendered some jobs unnecessary, led to massive workforce reductions in many industries, particularly steel, auto, garment, and electronics. This corporate restructuring affected blue-collar worker first and tended to be described simply a layoffs. By the time the restructuring hit the white-collar workforce, the practice had acquired another name: downsizing.

The downsizing trend alarmed people because when long-time employees los their jobs, that loss forever altered the faces of families, companies, and communities. Despite its unpopularity, downsizing became a part of many companies strategic planning. In 1997, for example Eastman Kodak announced plans to drop 10,000 employees from its ranks in an effort to cut $1 billion from its annual expenses. In 1998 Chase Manhattan cut about 3,000 employees from its administrative staff of 9,400, a move intended to shrink a cumbersome bureaucracy and reduce overhead; that same year, Xerox cut about 9,000 jobs when its expenses were determined to be much higher than those of its competitors. By 1999 more than 3.4 million jobs had been cut from Fortune 500 companies.

Downsizing changed white-collar workers' attitudes toward their jobs. In the past people had joined a company for life; they took a job when they were young and worked within the same company until they retired or died. Traditionally, employees stayed with a job 30 or 40 years, offering hard work and loyalty in exchange for an unwritten, but understood, lifetime of employment and retirement benefits. The practice of downsizing, combined with other changes in the marketplace, altered that thinking; long-term, stable employee–employer relationships gave way to short-term, contingent ones. Few employees now expect to stay within the same company all their lives.

Sometimes downsizing has offered advantages to the remaining employees. With communications streamlined, operations more flexible, and middle managers gone, rank-and-file workers were asked to take on managerial responsibilities and to be involved in team thinking and decision-making. General Electric chief executive

In Washington, D.C., workers protest against high unemployment in 1992. ("Read my lips" was an oft-used slogan of the George H. W. Bush administration, 1989–1993).

officer Jack Welch proposed eliminating 170,000 positions, and he announced that future employees would have only conditional employment but would be provided with the best training and professional development available.

Over time, corporations learned that downsizing was not only a menacing word but also could be an ineffective strategy. In light of the complexities of the marketplace, the elimination of jobs did not by itself improve cost-effectiveness or increase efficiency. Furthermore, downsizing destabilized organizations by destroying the morale and trust of employees and the community. The practice began to be reevaluated by management experts, who suggest that it be done with greater care than in the 1990s, mainly because of the widely recognized negative effect on worker morale. More positive-sounding words like—*rightsizing, realigning, and reengineering*—began to be used. All of the terms refer to broad-based, long-range structural changes made by corporations to improve their competitiveness in the emerging global and technological marketplace.

Further Reading

Carter, Tony. *The Aftermath of Reengineering: Downsizing and Corporate Performance.* New York: Hayworth Press, 1999.

Gowing, Marilyn K,. John D. Kraft, and James Campbell Quick, eds. *The New Organizational Reality: Downsizing, Restructuring, and Revitalization.* Washington, D.C.: American Psychological Association, 1997.

—*Karen Ehrle*

Charles Carter, an employee of the Arthur Andersen accounting firm, confronts what was left behind after massive layoffs. In the wake of the accounting scandals of 2001–2002, Andersen shrunk its Houston headquarters by more than two-thirds.

See also:
Management; Management
Theory.

Drucker, Peter

1909–
Management theorist

Peter Ferdinand Drucker, a management consultant, author, teacher, and lecturer, promoted the most influential management ideas of the twentieth century. Drucker has been called the father of management, a social ecologist, and a philosopher who has examined nearly every element of twentieth-century life.

Drucker came to the United States in his late 20s. He was born in 1909 in Vienna, Austria. Drucker's father was an economist and lawyer; his mother had studied medicine. Each week his parents held dinner parties for local intellectuals—for example, young Drucker was introduced to Sigmund Freud—providing the young man a stimulating learning environment.

While in fourth grade at a progressive private school, Drucker was made responsible for his own learning. His teacher required him to record what he expected to learn each week; at the week's conclusion he compared the results against those goals. Drucker showed promise as a writer, a talent encouraged by his teacher who required him to write two compositions every week. From the experience of this

*Management guru
Peter Drucker circa 1953.*

supportive teaching, Drucker developed a personal credo that he has shared with executives for more than 50 years: focus on what people can do, not what they cannot do.

Drucker left Vienna at age 17, enrolling at Hamburg University in Germany while also working for an export firm that sold hardware to India. He later transferred to Frankfurt University, earning a doctorate in public and international law in 1931. While a student, he accepted an offer to be the financial writer for Frankfurt's largest daily newspaper, *The Frankfurter General-Anzeiger.*

In 1933 Drucker fled Germany after one of his essays was banned and burned by the Nazi government. He took a job as an economist for an international bank in London. In 1937 he decided to relocate to what he called "future-facing" America, serving as an adviser to a group of British banks and also working as a correspondent for several British newspapers, including *The Financial Times.* He published an influential study of Nazi power called *The End of Economic Man: A Study of the New Totalitarianism* in 1939.

In the 1940s Drucker discovered that he was more interested in the behavior of people than he was in commodities and began to study management, particularly organizations. His earliest management study, *The Concept of the Corporation* (1946), was a scholarly reflection on General Motors. Drucker also became a professor of philosophy and politics at Bennington College in Vermont. He teaches, he says, to discover what he thinks.

Over his 60-year career, Drucker has published 31 books (two of them novels), most still in print and widely translated. Written in accessible, straightforward language, the books discuss his views on industrial organization, management, leadership development, the culture of business, employee motivation, strategy, and other topics.

Although Drucker claims never to make predictions, he possesses an amazing ability to spot trends early; for example, in the early 1950s he was among the first to announce that business would be thoroughly transformed by computer technology, and in 1961 he speculated about Japan's rise as an economic power.

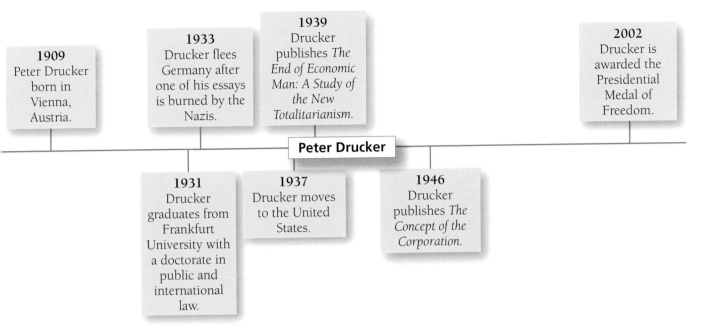

1909 Peter Drucker born in Vienna, Austria.

1933 Drucker flees Germany after one of his essays is burned by the Nazis.

1939 Drucker publishes *The End of Economic Man: A Study of the New Totalitarianism.*

2002 Drucker is awarded the Presidential Medal of Freedom.

Peter Drucker

1931 Drucker graduates from Frankfurt University with a doctorate in public and international law.

1937 Drucker moves to the United States.

1946 Drucker publishes *The Concept of the Corporation.*

In 1954 Drucker published *The Practice of Management,* practically inventing management as a discipline, which he believes feeds off economics, psychology, mathematics, political theory, history, and philosophy. He determined that the book would be a road map for managers, who at that time were given little management training or adequate supervisory tools.

Many of Drucker's theories have been put to practical use throughout the business world, including management through the setting of objectives rather than by control, and marketing as a central management task. As a consultant, he has specialized in strategy and policy for businesses, nonprofits, and government agencies around the globe. He is perhaps most famous for his direct criticisms of management, acknowledging that clients consider him a management "insultant."

Drucker believes that the most important asset of any organization is its people, and that the task of management is to make employees more capable of working together, while making their strengths effective and their weaknesses irrelevant. Drucker's creed has always been "Value and service first, profit later. Maximizing profit, perhaps never."

In the 1970s Drucker was named the Clarke Professor of Social Sciences and Management at the Claremont Graduate School in California. He also was a popular, monthly columnist for the editorial page of *The Wall Street Journal,* a tenure that would last for 20 years. In recognition of his accomplishments, in 2002 Drucker was awarded the Presidential Medal of Freedom, the highest civilian honor given by the United States.

Further Reading
Beatty, Jack. *The World according to Peter Drucker.* New York: Broadway Books, 1999.
Drucker, Peter F. *Adventures of a Bystander.* New York: John Wiley & Sons, 1998.
———. *The Essential Drucker.* New York: HarperBusiness, 2001.

—*Sheri Rehwoldt*

Some of Peter Drucker's Contributions

- Made management a discipline.
- Introduced key concepts including management by objective and decentralization.
- Identified the significance of knowledge workers in the modern economy
- Predicted the move to a global economy.
- Emphasized the importance of nonprofits, or the social sector, in addressing social problems.
- Foresaw the importance of institutional investors in late-twentieth-century capitalism.
- Predicted the trend toward privatization.
- Defined entrepreneurship as finding innovations to meet unmet needs.
- Emphasized the impact of technology, demographics, and education on the effectiveness of all organizations.
- Stressed business as an organ of society.

E-Business

E-business is a term used to describe business conducted through the Internet. In some business and industry sectors, e-business has transformed the processes by which business is conducted.

The term *e-business* is sometimes used interchangeably with *e-commerce*, but the terms are not identical in meaning. In contrast to e-business, e-commerce focuses more narrowly on conducting transactions via the Internet, not necessarily on integrating the Internet into a company's overall business strategy. E-commerce has existed in the form of electronic data interchange (EDI) since the 1960s, long before private companies gained access to the Internet. EDI involves a direct computer-to-computer exchange of documents, but it requires the use of standardized formats, limiting the scope of its applications. EDI still has valuable uses, but its value is likely to continue to decline. In the automobile industry, for example, manufacturers have used EDI to connect with their suppliers but have developed a joint e-business exchange known as Covisint (http://www.covisint.com) for the same purpose. A Covisint press release indicated that from January 2001 to August 2001, automakers used the exchange to purchased more than $129 billion in parts and raw materials from their suppliers.

E-business has evolved from a virtually nonexistent concept in the mid-1990s to a multibillion-dollar venture. Many observers believe that e-business will revolutionize business practices, play a strong role in determining which companies will survive, and shape relationships among individual consumers, employees, and companies.

Business-to-Consumer E-Business

E-business initiatives can be observed in several areas of business practice. Of these areas, business-to-consumer (B2C) transactions have been especially visible.

B2C transactions involve the marketing, sale, and delivery of products and services to consumers via the Internet. Some of the most visible and well-known business-to-consumer ventures include Amazon.com (http://www.amazon.com), the online auction marketplace Ebay (http://www.ebay.com), and Priceline.com (http://www.priceline.com). Almost any consumer good or service one might imagine—from personal insurance and online banking to automobiles, pet food, and furniture—has been or is currently sold via the Internet. Early on, many B2C retailers were not traditional retail companies or manufacturers of consumer products but rather stand-alone ventures known as the dot-coms.

More established, traditional retailers and service providers have since developed e-business capabilities. In some instances, traditional retailers and service providers had been reluctant to establish a major Web presence for fear it would undercut the success of their established channels for reaching consumers—channels they had built up over many years, at great cost and effort. For example, a traditional stock brokerage firm would need to consider whether it should allow customers to make their own trades online in exchange for transaction fees or if doing so would hurt its employees—stockbrokers and traders who earn commissions for trades and establish valuable personal relationships with customers. A dot-com online trading service like E-trade had no such concerns.

Traditional providers of products and services have made use of trusted brand names, reputations for customer service, and knowledge of their industries in their efforts to launch e-business operations. Traditional banks have developed online banking capabilities, and lending companies offer online loan applications. Traditional bookseller Barnes & Noble has established a formidable online presence (http://www.barnesandnoble.com) to compete with Amazon.com in selling books, music, and even online educational courses. Taking a different approach, Toys R Us has entered into an alliance with Amazon.com to establish its e-business presence.

Two Kinds of E-Business

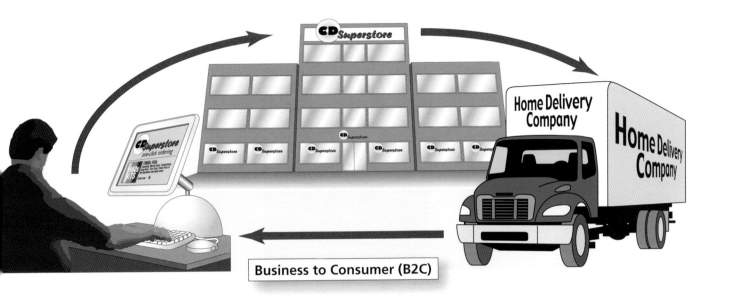

Business to Consumer (B2C)

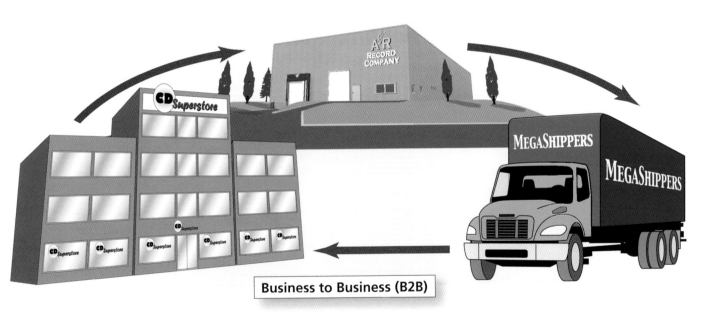

Business to Business (B2B)

A key technology that has driven the development of B2C e-business is integration of Web sites (the visible interface for consumers) with internal corporate databases. These databases are used to gather data from consumers as they visit a Web site and to incorporate those data into internal business data systems. At the same time, data can be drawn from these and other data systems and brought seamlessly into the content consumers see when they visit a Web site. One result is the ability to analyze customer spending and browsing patterns, customize what a consumer sees on future trips to a Web site based on past visits and buying habits, and, in some cases, adjust prices instantaneously based on knowledge about the consumer (a tactic often called dynamic pricing). These strategies are part of customer relationship management (CRM), a term used to describe a broad spectrum of functions and applications aimed at fostering customer loyalty through improved sales, marketing, and customer service.

Despite these promising applications, integrating Web sites and e-business software

E-business is friendly to small firms. Raj Yersai (left) and Sumit Kapur founded an online auction site to sell American products in India.

concern is whether sales via e-business should be taxed, and if so, by what governmental unit. Last, observers are concerned about the use of e-business capabilities to circumvent government regulation (examples include offshore gambling operations that make online games available to persons living in the United States, or sites that allow purchase of prescription drugs without face-to-face consultation with a physician). All these topics will require further attention from policy makers in the future.

Business-to-Business

While the B2C impact of e-business has been very visible to the general public, many believe business-to-business (B2B) transactions will constitute a larger sector, eventually dwarfing B2C in dollar terms. Determining the true size of e-business as an industry is difficult, but estimates for global B2B e-business predict a growth rate of approximately 83 percent per year since 2001, reaching $8.5 trillion by 2005.

Why is B2B expected to be so large? Most companies rely on a network of business relationships with other companies. Manufacturers have business relationships with suppliers of raw materials, components, and services; with companies that distribute their products to customers; and they have direct relationships with some customers. Similarly, hospitals may conduct business with a host of suppliers—pharmaceutical and medical device companies, linen suppliers, and food companies. They also conduct business with other medical service providers like physician clinics, laboratories, and diagnostic imaging centers. They conduct business with payers—insurance companies, government programs, and individuals.

E-business offers tools for streamlining business communications and for sharing information in ways that promise a more timely business process, better information for making decisions, and the prospect of creating new business relationships. At least a few of these e-business tools are somewhat similar in concept to those used for B2C e-business.

applications with internal databases and business processes has proven to be daunting for many companies. Tom Kaneshige notes in a December 2001 article, "Surviving CRM," that many CRM projects fail to meet expectations and that even minor problems with CRM systems can be quite damaging to the customer relationships they are intended to strengthen. Further, some products and services do not lend themselves readily to Internet applications. Consumers are more willing to purchase discounted airline tickets or music on compact disks over the Internet than they are to purchase a large piece of furniture without bouncing on the springs or an automobile without kicking the tires.

Beyond implementation problems and product applicability, the rapid growth of B2C e-business also has posed particular problems for public policy and the legal system, which had not anticipated some uses of the Internet. Many legal issues concerning copyright protection, contracts, and privacy issues related to the use of data gathered about consumers remain unresolved. Another area of indecision and

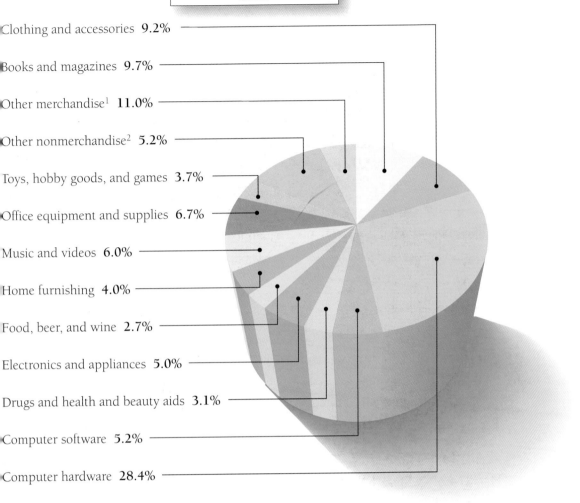

**E-Commerce Sales
by Type of Merchandise
2000**

Clothing and accessories **9.2%**

Books and magazines **9.7%**

Other merchandise[1] **11.0%**

Other nonmerchandise[2] **5.2%**

Toys, hobby goods, and games **3.7%**

Office equipment and supplies **6.7%**

Music and videos **6.0%**

Home furnishing **4.0%**

Food, beer, and wine **2.7%**

Electronics and appliances **5.0%**

Drugs and health and beauty aids **3.1%**

Computer software **5.2%**

Computer hardware **28.4%**

[1]Includes merchandise such as collectibles, souvenirs, auto parts, hardware, lawn and garden equipment, and jewelry.
[2]Includes nonmerchandise receipts such as auction commissions, customer training, customer support, advertising, and shipping and handling.
Source: Bureau of the Census, *2000 Annual Retail Trade Survey,* Washington, D.C.

Customer relationship management is used in the B2B arena to help companies gather better information about their customers' ongoing needs or interests. One goal is to manage accounts and orders so that managers may more readily understand them; another is to provide forecasts of demand so that production and service-provision levels may be altered accordingly, and overall customer service improved. Some CRM applications now extend beyond the Internet into the wireless device environment, so that roving staff can enter and receive data using handheld digital devices like pocket computers and personal digital assistants. Unfortunately, the more entry points for data, the greater the risk of erroneous data entry, potentially undermining the intended purpose of having more information available for better decision making.

Supply chain management (SCM) is another popular area for e-business projects. SCM seeks to ensure that needed products, parts, or materials will be purchased efficiently, at favorable prices, and that they will be available when needed for production or sale. SCM encompasses many activities; one example is collaborative logistics and shipping. Companies shipping products from one point to another are often charged the cost to ship a whole truckload even when their product fills only half the space in the

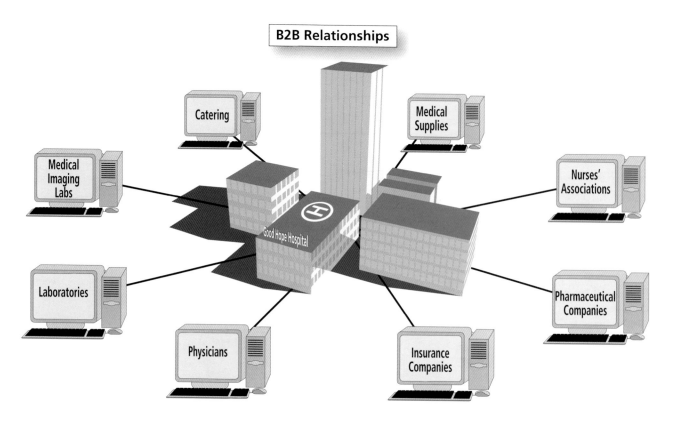

B2B Relationships

truck. This drives up the unit price for each product shipped. Online shipping exchanges like Nistevo (http://www.nistevo.com) help companies coordinate and share truckloads, so that several companies shipping goods over the same route can use one truck and split the shipping cost among them, thus lowering unit costs.

Online product configuration and collaborative design applications make designing over the Internet possible for engineers from one or more companies. As manufacturers of complex, highly engineered products often work with many parts and systems suppliers, the process of finding and ordering those parts, or making sure the parts are designed to suit their specific needs, can be burdensome and time-consuming. Web-based configurators, like one offered by Technicon (http://www.technicon.com), can give prospective purchasers detailed product information and sophisticated three-dimensional drawings from a manufacturer's or distributor's Web site at any time. Such configurators also reduce errors and redundant tasks in the design process and increase the speed with which a product can be designed and delivered.

In addition to these individual tools or applications, industry portals and exchanges offer a more extensive B2B model that attempts to serve entire industries but with somewhat different emphases. Portals seek to be the primary and first source of information for persons and organizations participating in an industry. They generate revenue through sponsors, charging for access to key content, or selling advertising space on their portal sites. Some portals, for example, Benefitslink (http://www.benefits.com) for the employee benefits industry, or drkoop.com (http://www.drkoop.com) for health information, are freestanding Internet-only companies, often with corporate sponsors and members. Other portals, such as Manufacturing.Net (http://www.manufacturing.net), are sponsored by publishers using the portals to extend their print-based businesses to the Internet.

The goal of exchanges, or marketplaces, is to become the sole or primary place where B2B transactions take place within an industry. These transactions might take place in an online bidding or auction environment, or they might occur where potential business partners meet online and use Web configuration and collaboration, or project management ools made available by the exchange or marketplace to cement business relationships. Online marketplaces and exchanges serve various industries. Some marketplace sponsors focus on specific industries, for example FoodService.com (http://www.foodbuy.com) or the food service industry or PetroChemNet (http://www.petrochem.net) for the petrochemical industry. Some others, including FreeMarkets (http://www.freemarkets.com), seek to provide marketplaces serving multiple industries.

The marketplace and exchange concept has its drawbacks. For example, in some industries, manufacturers have been reluctant to participate in a transaction environment that threatens to erode brand image and reduce competition to a price-only basis by placing the purchase of complex products on a level comparable to that of choosing a toothpick supplier. Also exchanges can threaten existing business relationships among manufacturers and distributors. Distributors sell and provide services related to manufacturer products and fear being cut out of the business by marketplaces. Manufacturers, who depend on distributors, are sometimes reluctant to disturb these relationships by pursuing sales through exchanges and marketplaces.

Some industries are too small to support competing exchanges and marketplaces. Exchanges and marketplaces, which make a relatively small fee per transaction, must achieve a very large number of transactions to recoup their costs and make a profit.

Regardless of the sector, the relative infancy of e-business and rapid advancements in supporting technology suggest that e-business can be expected to play a growing role in shaping the conduct of business and the behavior of consumers. E-business can generate efficiencies and productivity growth, contributing to improvements in standards of living around the world. At the same time, areas of the world lacking in technology infrastructure may suffer by being left further behind. Changes in business processes will mean that some jobs disappear while new ones emerge. E-business can support trends toward globalization of a vast range of industries,

along with decentralization of corporate workforces, by making possible business transactions by people and organizations separated by vast distances. At the same time, something may be lost by decreasing face-to-face interaction, and the growth of e-business in some areas may be limited by a persistent interest of some individuals in maintaining a sense of closeness in business relationships.

The uncertainty associated with e-business is not in itself a new phenomenon. It has appeared before, at the beginning of other new technologies including the printing press and the airplane. Those technologies changed business and personal lives profoundly. E-business shows a similar potential for transformation.

Further Reading

Kaneshige, Tom. "Surviving CRM." *Line56*, December 2001, 44.

Rayport, Jeffrey F., and Bernard J. Jaworski. *E-Commerce*. Boston: McGraw-Hill/Irwin, 2002.

Shelly, Gary B., Thomas J. Cashman, and Judy A. Serwatka. *Business Data Communications: Introductory Concepts and Techniques*. Boston: Thomson Learning, 2001.

Tapscott, Don, David Ticoll, and Alex Lowy. *Digital Capital: Harnessing the Power of Business Webs*. London: Nicholas Brealey, 2000.

United Nations Conference on Trade and Development, Electronic Commerce Branch. "E-Commerce and Development Report 2002." http://www.unctad.org/ecommerce (January 7, 2003).

—*Peter Alles*

Web Resources for E-Business

www.e-businessworld.com provides news and resources for the international e-business world.

ebusiness.ittoolbox.com provides a virtual e-business community for information technology professionals.

www.news.com, maintained by the firm CNET, is a good source of articles about the e-business industry and the Internet in general.

www.crmindustry.com is an informational portal for the customer relationship management industry.

www.fcw.com/geb focuses on resources for government e-businesses.

Frank Lynn & Associates consulting firm has a list of public exchanges and marketplaces at www.franklynn.com/ebusiness/index.html

The Wisconsin Health Information Network (WHIN) provides a diagram showing how a central interchange might be used to coordinate all the interconnected data-sharing required for health care e-business at www.whin.net/about_us/glance.html

Economic Growth

Economic growth is a measure of a nation's progress and wealth, and it determines the standard of living of its citizens. For these reasons, growth is important when judging the performance of an economy and is at the center of both economic debates and political events across the world.

Economic growth is defined as an increase in an economy's ability to produce goods and services and is commonly measured by gross domestic product (GDP), the value of the total amount of goods and services produced by the economy during a specific period. A nation with a growing GDP is producing more goods and services than in the previous year and thus is experiencing economic growth. Such growth is associated with stable or increasing employment, rising wages, political stability, and a rising standard of living. A nation with shrinking GDP likely has the opposite conditions.

Economists do not have a complete understanding of economic growth. They do agree that the central underlying idea is productivity, which is defined as the amount of goods and services that can be produced for each unit of time. Adam Smith, the founder of modern economics, developed the concept of economic growth in a famous passage from his landmark 1776 work *The Wealth of Nations* in which he discussed the example of a pin factory. Smith theorized that, working alone, one person could make no more than 20 pins in one day of work. Smith then explained how the manufacturer could increase output by introducing better tools and by training workers to do specific tasks, a process called specialization of labor or division of labor. The result of Smith's hypothetical example was an increase in daily production from 20 pins per person working alone to 48,000 produced by 10 workers.

The division of labor results in numerous benefits. Consumers gain as production increases and prices decrease with the increase in supply. The entrepreneur benefits from increased sales, while the workers can earn raises because of their increased contribution to profits.

Resources vs. Gross Domestic Product 2000

Russia
Resources: Wide natural resource base including major deposits of oil, natural gas, coal, many strategic minerals, and timber

GDP per capita $7,700

Hong Kong
Resources: Outstanding deepwater harbor, feldspar

GDP per capita $25,400

Nigeria
Resources: Natural gas, petroleum, tin, columbite, iron ore, coal, limestone, lead, zinc, arable land

GDP per capita $950

Japan
Resources: Negligible mineral resources, fish

GDP per capita $24,900

Source: Central Intelligence Agency, *CIA Factbook*, Washington, D.C.

Encouraging Economic Growth

Smith's work contributed to the understanding of how to create growth. Economists generally agree that the key elements are physical and human capital, investment, infrastructure, and private property rights.

The first two are prominent in the pin factory example. Physical capital is defined as tools used to produce and distribute goods and services. Human capital refers to the skills and experience of workers in production. Clearly, as both physical and human capital become more abundant, production will increase and economic growth will be encouraged.

Investment is the use of resources today so that they will enable greater production in the future. For example, when an entrepreneur builds a new factory or buys new equipment, she is contributing to economic growth in the future. The key to investment is savings: if investors are confident in the future, they will delay current spending to invest, in hopes of greater returns later. Thus, both savings and investment encourage growth.

Infrastructure encompasses a country's transportation, education, communication, and financial systems. Because these reduce the cost of doing business, they encourage economic growth. For example, an excellent highway system lowers transportation costs, thereby increasing profit opportunities and encouraging businesses to take risks. Each part of infrastructure is an example in how investing now can result in economic growth in the future.

A common misperception is that natural resources, for example coal, iron, and steel, play a prominent part in economic growth. Economists have found that they are not very important (see illustration on page 388). For example, both Russia and Nigeria are rich in natural resources, including oil and gas, which can be very profitable to sell. Hong Kong and Japan, by contrast, are endowed with few natural resources. Yet Hong Kong and Japan have far higher GDP per capita (the average amount of economic production per person in a nation). Hong Kong and

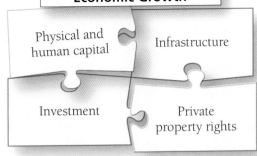

Key Elements in Creating Economic Growth

Physical and human capital

Infrastructure

Investment

Private property rights

Japan are far more economically productive than Russia and Nigeria. Infrastructure, especially access to education, has contributed to Hong Kong and Japan's GDP.

Another part of the answer to the puzzle of economic growth lies in a nation's treatment of property rights. Property rights allow individuals to control and reap benefits from things of value that they own. This includes the right to freedom of choice concerning management of the property, including selling it, buying more, and so on. Economics is based on the idea that individuals are motivated by greed and will therefore manage their property to maximize their self-interest, in other words, profits. In theory, private property creates an incentive to succeed economically.

Private property rights are almost universally weak in poor countries, including Russia and Nigeria. In countries with weak property rights, generally a rich minority dominates the government and the judicial system. Those in power tend to ignore the property rights of the poor majority and manipulate the police and legal system through corruption. One immediate result is that the poor lack incentives to work hard, because any property they earn is subject to confiscation by others. A result is that the country remains poor.

Governments and Economic Growth

As a way to best support economic growth, Adam Smith argued for the concept of laissez-faire, a policy of minimizing government interference in the economy. Nevertheless, the worldwide trend since the late 1800s has been one of increasing government involvement in economic activity.

Economic growth, rarely reliable and predictable, occurs during a process called the business cycle. The business cycle has periods of growth, or expansion, and slower or even negative growth, called contraction. Governments have developed several tools to help stabilize the business cycle and encourage sustainable economic growth. The most important of these are the central banks; in the United States, the central banks are called the Federal Reserve System.

Central banks promote economic stability by implementing a monetary policy. Such policy involves controlling the money supply and changing interest rates to promote or reduce economic activity. Thus, the central banks can speed or slow economic growth and reduce the severity of swings in the business cycle.

Governments can also use fiscal policy, or government spending, as a tool for managing economic growth. John Maynard Keynes advocated government spending as a solution to the Great Depression, arguing that it could regulate the business cycle. For example, if a nation is entering a recession, the government may increase spending or cut taxes to reduce unemployment and increase funds in the hands of individuals; such funds would be available for spending.

Problems with Growth

Economic growth is not without its negatives. It can cause inflation and does not occur without social cost. Inflation is a rise in prices caused by an increase in the money supply. These changes are positively associated with economic growth, meaning that as the economy expands, the money supply as well as prices will rise. However, uncontrolled inflation is very unhealthy for an economy. As prices increase, consumers have an incentive to spend their money immediately—rather than save—before the goods they desire become even more expensive. Consumers also tend to demand higher wages to preserve their purchasing power. Both acts serve to exacerbate the inflation.

Countries with the Highest and Lowest Gross National Income per Capita 2001

Highest GNI per Capita		Lowest GNI per Capita	
1.	Luxembourg	1.	Ethiopia
2.	Liechtenstein	2.	Burundi
3.	Switzerland	3.	Sierra Leone
4.	Japan	4.	Guinea-Bissau
5.	Norway	5.	Tajikistan
6.	Bermuda	6.	Niger
7.	United States	7.	Malawi
8.	Denmark	8.	Eritrea
9.	Cayman Islands	9.	Chad
10.	Iceland	10.	Mozambique

Source: World Bank, GNI Per Capita 2001, http://www.worldbank.org/data/databytopic/GNIPC.pdf (January 7, 2002).

Critics point out that economic growth is not always completely positive; for example, the construction of more factories can mean more jobs but also more pollution.

The accepted medicine for inflation is for the central bank to raise interest rates, slowing the economy and reducing the inflation. Thus, the only cure for serious inflation is to send the nation into a recession, deliberately increasing unemployment. This very unpopular policy is the reason for many central banks being independent of political control.

The other drawback of economic growth is social cost: growth can be very disruptive. The quest for higher business profits through increasing productivity and creating new goods and services is the basis of capitalism. The cost of this system is that the new and improved products result in the displacement of established producers, often resulting in the bankruptcy of companies and unemployment for their workers.

The manufacturing sector of the U.S. economy provides a clear example. The trend since World War II has been a decline in highly paid factory jobs as companies relocate abroad to take advantage of cheaper labor

Overall employment in the United States has increased, as manufacturing jobs have been replaced by lower-paying service jobs.

costs. Many industries once dominated by American manufacturers, including the manufacture of television sets, steel, and textiles, have mostly disappeared in the United States.

One result of this trend has been pressure on the American middle class. Earning higher wages requires more education than it did in the 1950s, while more households earn dual income (both husband and wife working) to preserve spending power. Overall employment in the United States, however, has actually increased despite the loss of jobs in some industries, though the jobs being created tend to be lower-paid service-sector jobs.

Accordingly, many critics charge that economic growth is misrepresented as a measure of progress. They assert that definite costs are associated with growth and that those costs are not included in the standard measure of GDP. For example, economic growth often results in increased pollution as more factories are built. More pollution can lead to increased illness, destruction of natural resources, and other harmful effects.

Critics contend that the GDP is a flawed measure because it incorporates neither these negatives nor any quality-of-life measurements.

They suggest that additional measures, including poverty rates, pollution, and wealth distribution, be used to accurately measure the economic progress of a nation.

One result of these critiques is that measurement of economic growth is increasingly controversial. Ideas about balancing growth with environmental concerns, equity, and other factors are becoming more accepted. The increased scrutiny of growth by both academics and politicians has resulted in the world's economies being more stable, better understood, and less prone to destructive boom and bust cycles.

Further Reading

Heilbroner, Robert. *The Worldly Philosophers: The Lives, Times, and Ideas of the Great Economic Thinkers.* Rev. 7th ed. New York: Simon & Schuster, 1999.

McEachern, William A. *Economics: A Contemporary Introduction.* 2nd ed. Cincinnati, Ohio: South-Western College Publishing, 2000.

Reich, Robert. *The Work of Nations: Preparing Ourselves for 21st Century Capitalism.* New York: Vintage Books, 1992.

Thurow, Lester C., and Robert Heilbroner. *Economics Explained: Everything You Need to Know about How the Economy Works and Where It Is Going.* New York: Touchstone Publishing, 1999.

—*David Long*

Economic Opportunity Act

By the early 1960s the United States was the richest nation in the world. Material goods like televisions, appliances, and cars were common in American middle-class households, and young people could attend high school and college without worrying about working to help support their parents. Outside the middle class, however, a significant number of American families were plagued by limited opportunity; many were poor and poverty-stricken in a land of plenty. In the 1960s, 10 million families earned up to $60 per week with nearly two-thirds of them earning only $40 per week. The disparity between families in poverty living among families of affluence led to the passage of the Economic Opportunity Act of 1964.

The Economic Opportunity Act was the first salvo in what became known as the War on Poverty. The act established the Office of Economic Opportunity (OEO) in the executive office of the president of the United States. The act's roots dated to

1924, to the Conference for Progressive Political Action's platform, which stated, "every generation must wage a new war for freedom against new forces that seek through new devices to enslave mankind." The conference's platform also called for a program of public service, which became the programmatic basis for the Economic Opportunity Act.

The Economic Opportunity Act established institutions not only to combat existing poverty but also to launch initiatives to prevent an increase. The act focused on the specific needs of different groups of people, rather than attempting to develop one broad strategy for all the nation's economically disadvantaged. Programs addressed education with projects like Head Start (for preschool children) and Adult Basic Education; health care with community health and family planning centers; guidance for young people through foster grandparenting and summer youth programs; and local economies through loans to small businesses and farmers, as well as local economic development projects.

The Economic Opportunity Act identified six core groups at risk: children in

See also:
Affirmative Action; Equal Employment Opportunity Commission.

In the same year the Economic Opportunity Act was passed, children play in a North Carolina slum, in the shadow of high-rise buildings.

AN ACT
To mobilize the human and financial resources of the Nation to combat poverty
in the United States.

Be it enacted by the Senate and House of Representatives of the United States of America in Congress assembled. That this Act may be cited as the "Economic Opportunity Act of 1964."

FINDINGS AND DECLARATION OF PURPOSE

SEC. 2. Although the economic well-being and prosperity of the United States have progressed to a level surpassing any achieved in world history, and although these benefits are widely shared throughout the Nation, poverty continues to be the lot of a substantial number of our people. The United States can achieve its full economic and social potential as a nation only if every individual has the opportunity to contribute to the full extent of his capabilities and to participate in the workings of our society. It is, therefore, the policy of the United States to eliminate the paradox of poverty in the midst of plenty in this Nation by opening to everyone the opportunity for education and training, the opportunity to work, and the opportunity to live in decency and dignity. It is the purpose of this Act to strengthen, supplement, and coordinate efforts in furtherance of that policy.

poverty, ethnic minorities, the bypassed (dislocated industrial workers), the rural poor, fatherless (female-headed) families, and the aged. Children in poverty were chosen as a key target group in an attempt to break the intergenerational cycle of poverty. The Job Corps was a boarding school–type program created for young adults, many of whom were high school dropouts, to teach them marketable skills. Inculcating the participants with a positive view of regular and meaningful work was a central component of this initiative. Other programs included the Work Training Program and Work-Study Program, which were also substantially focused on instilling the work ethic and the respect for the value of work in the participants.

The community action component of the Economic Opportunity Act was designed to help communities develop their own strategies for economic self-sufficiency through advocacy, educational programs, and participation in policy making and the institutions that directly affected their lives. To that end, more than 1,000 Community Action Agencies (CAAs) were created to manage programs and distribute funds at the local level. These federal funds came with statutory requirements mandating a specific level of participation by the poor in all decision making. Poor people, for the first time, began to be a significant presence on boards and commissions and have their voices heard when setting policies for distribution of resources in their communities.

Beginning in 1972, EOA programs were gradually transferred to other federal depart-

President Lyndon Johnson displays the Economic Opportunity Act, which he signed on August 20, 1964.

ments, including Health, Education, and Labor. The Community Service Amendments of 1974 replaced the CAAs with the Community Services Administration, which was itself abolished in 1981. CAAs, however, still manage programs for local communities.

Several other programs that came out of the Economic Opportunity Act of 1964 are still in place. The Volunteers in Service to America (VISTA) program was merged with the Peace Corps in the 1970s. In the 1990s VISTA became a part of the Clinton administration's Americorps, which engages more than 50,000 Americans as volunteers in economic development programs, day care, affordable home construction for the poor, neighborhood safety programs, and a host of other efforts. The Work-Study Program for students enrolled in postsecondary education provides millions of dollars to deserving students annually, allowing them to earn money to pay for their education. The Job Corps continues to target at-risk youth and young adults, providing them with work skills and teaching positive values.

An Americorps volunteer tutors a schoolgirl in Lafayette, Louisiana.

Further Reading

Karger, Howard Jacob, and David Stoesz. *American Social Welfare Policy: A Pluralist Approach.* 4th ed. Boston: Allyn & Bacon, 2002.

Katz, Michael B. *The Undeserving Poor: From the War on Poverty to the War on Welfare.* New York: Pantheon Books, 1990.

The War on Poverty: The Economic Opportunity Act of 1964. Washington, D.C.: Government Printing Office, 1964.

—*Walter C. Farrell, Jr., Douglas Bradshaw Bynum, and Reneé Sartin Kirby*

See also:
Assembly Line; Division of Labor.

Economies of Scale

Economies of scale occur when a business's average cost of production declines as its output increases. Economies of scale enable a business to produce a greater amount at a lower per-unit cost. Economies of scale arise from the nature of the technology employed and the efficiencies gained by large-scale production. Large economies of scale can have a significant effect on a firm's business strategy and on market structure.

Businesses of all kinds transform resources, or factors of production, into some kind of output, either a good or a service. These factors of production include labor, capital (factories, machinery, and equipment), and raw materials or natural resources. Increasing output requires some increase in resources, so the total cost of production rises as more inputs are purchased and output rises. However, total cost need not necessarily rise in proportion to output, and this creates the possibility of economies of scale. For example, if a firm is able to double its output (a 100 percent increase) while incurring only an 80 percent increase in costs, then the average cost of production will actually decline. Imagine a firm making 1,000 units of output at a total cost of $10,000, or $10 per unit. If output rises to 2,000 units while total cost increases to $18,000, then the average cost of production falls to $9 per unit; the firm enjoys economies of scale and a higher profit.

The technology employed in the production process is fundamental in determining whether economies of scale will be achieved. An important source of economies of scale lies in a production phenomenon called increasing returns to scale. Increasing returns to scale occur when raising the use of all resources by the same percentage leads to an even larger percentage increase in output. Increasing returns to scale in production result in economies of scale in costs. For example, if increasing all resources by 80 percent leads to a 100 percent increase in production, then output goes up faster than costs, with a corresponding drop in average cost.

Why might increasing returns to scale result in higher production? The most common answer involves the ability to employ resources in highly specialized ways that can increase the productivity of these resources. A manufacturing firm, for example, may find that when it employs more workers, each worker can perform a more focused task better and productivity, or output per worker, rises. Henry Ford's use of the assembly line in the early days of automobile manufacturing took advantage of this highly productive division of labor.

Increasing returns to scale involves increasing of all resources proportionally. However, sometimes the optimal mix of resources changes at larger scales of operation, which can also result in economies of scale. For example, a manufacturing firm might find it needs only 50 percent more workers to staff a production facility that is twice as large as its old one. The new labor-to-capital ratio might reduce the average cost of production at the higher output level, resulting in economies of scale. Similarly, physical capital can sometimes be more productive at larger scales of operation, usually the result of certain physical characteristics. A pipeline for transporting liquid or gas, for example, might be more efficient in a bigger size. Doubling the

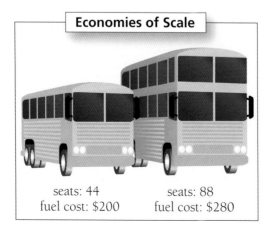

Economies of Scale

seats: 44
fuel cost: $200

seats: 88
fuel cost: $280

The double-decker bus doubles the number of seats but without doubling fuel costs.

circumference of the pipeline may double its cost to the firm, but doubling the circumference much more than doubles the volume of material that can flow through the pipeline.

A similar phenomenon occurs when the optimal production technique requires some initial input or start-up expenditure to make the process work. For example, a transmission and distribution system must be in place before electrical power can begin to be distributed in a large network. The large initial cost of the system can be spread out over more buyers as the customer base expands, thus reducing the cost per unit.

Economies of scale affect business behavior and the structure of the marketplace. In an industry in which firms can achieve significant economies of scale, small firms will typically have difficulty competing with larger firms because the small firms have a higher average cost of production. Such small firms often will

either have to grow to operate at a level that takes advantage of economies of scale or settle for low profits, perhaps even being forced out of business. Industries with very large economies of scale tend to become oligopolistic: only a few firms compete with one another, typically at large scales of operation.

The automobile manufacturing industry is an example of an oligopoly with important economies of scale. At the beginning of automobile manufacture in the United States, a number of firms sprang up, but automated production techniques and division of labor quickly resulted in economies of scale. Manufacturers became large producers, consolidated their operations by merging with other manufacturers, or went out of business. For most of the twentieth century, three or four major producers dominated American automobile manufacturing. At the beginning of the twenty-first century, consolidation among manufacturers around the world continued

Economies of scale are important for electricity companies; the high cost of establishing the generation and delivery systems can be spread among many customers.

The automobile industry was profoundly shaped by economies of scale.

to be the rule, resulting in a global oligopoly in which a relatively few huge manufacturers produce the vast majority of automobiles, and smaller producers struggle to survive.

Minimum efficient scale is defined as the level of output that must be reached to exhaust economies of scale. Beyond that level of production, no further cost advantage is derived from increasing the scale of production. In some cases, economies of scale are so large that no more than one firm can reach minimum efficient scale. In these situations having multiple firms compete would likely result in inefficient, high-cost production and an unstable market structure, until one firm succeeds in capturing enough market share to drive out competitors. These cases are sometimes called natural monopolies, because it often makes economic sense to have only one firm in the industry. Historically, public utilities, such as electric power and local telephone service providers, have been considered natural monopolies.

Further Reading

Heilbroner, Robert, and William Milberg. *The Making of Economic Society.* 11th ed. Upper Saddle River, N.J.: Prentice Hall, 2002.
Schiller, Bradley R. *Essentials of Economics.* 4th ed. Boston: McGraw-Hill/Irwin, 2002.

—*Randall E. Waldron*

Edison, Thomas Alva

1847–1931
Inventor

When a lightbulb goes on over a cartoon character's head to illustrate a good idea, it is probably because the inventor of the lightbulb, Thomas A. Edison, had more good ideas than anyone else. Mostly self-taught from the age of eight and virtually deaf from age 12, Edison invented many of the products that are intrinsic to life in developed countries.

Edison was born on February 11, 1847, in Milan, Ohio. According to his father, Edison asked too many questions. In 1854 the Edison family moved to Port Huron, Michigan, where the elder Edison began a lumber, grain, and feed business. Young Edison caught scarlet fever at age seven, and at age eight he began school. He did not get along well with his teacher, however, and his family was short of money, so his mother Nancy removed him from school and began teaching him at home. When he was nine she gave him a book about science experiments. At age 10 he built a home laboratory; at 11 he made himself a telegraph machine and practiced using Morse code; and at 12 he took a job selling food to passengers on a train that traveled between Port Huron and Detroit. He had begun by then to go deaf, probably as a result of the scarlet fever. At age 15 he began to patronize the Detroit Free Library, and he soon claimed to have read every book there.

In 1862 Edison chanced to come upon a three-year-old child playing on some train tracks in the path of a moving boxcar. Edison rescued the child, and the child's grateful father—the railroad stationmaster—taught Edison the craft of the telegraph operator. During the next few years, Edison worked intermittently as a telegraph operator, sometimes losing jobs because he was more interested in experimenting with the equipment than in performing his duties.

In debt and restless, Edison traveled to New York in 1870, eager to escape his creditors and to get close to the economic center of the country. In New York he visited a friend who worked at the Gold Indicator Company, which transmitted information about fluctuating gold prices to brokers. During Edison's visit the entire transmission system broke down. Nobody at the company could repair the transmission device. Edison fixed it, however, and the company hired him immediately. Later that year Edison also worked for Western Union, devising improvements for its stock ticker. With the $40,000 he was paid for that work, Edison set up a laboratory in New Jersey.

In 1876 he built another research laboratory, this one in Menlo Park, New Jersey.

See also:
General Electric; Patent;
Research and Development;
Utilities Industry.

Thomas Alva Edison in his laboratory.

The Menlo Park lab would become a model for industrial research laboratories in the twentieth century. By 1877, seven years after his arrival in New York, Edison had registered more than 200 patents, including one for the mimeograph machine, which he sold to A. B. Dick of Chicago.

In addition to inventing new products, Edison developed improvements for existing products. For Western Union, for example, he improved upon Alexander Graham Bell's telephone. Edison separated the telephone receiver and transmitter and also increased the range of the instrument. As he was deaf, Edison sometimes bit into the telephone wire on which he was working to "hear" through his teeth whether his modifications had actually improved transmission. In working on a way to record telephone calls, Edison also invented the phonograph, which he demonstrated for Congress in 1878; this extraordinary invention earned him the sobriquet of "Wizard of Menlo Park."

Electricity

In 1878 a traveling companion suggested that Edison look into producing light from electric current. In approaching the problem Edison sought to duplicate what the gas industry had achieved in delivering gas to individual homes. He wanted to deliver electricity to every home in a manner that would allow people to switch lights on and off in each room as needed. One problem was the bulb itself. No one had found a filament material that would glow brightly enough when electricity was passed through

it without also burning out quickly. Edison tested more than 1,600 materials before he found an answer in carbonized cotton thread. Later he found a better filament material in carbonized bamboo fiber.

During this time Edison and his team also improved dynamos (machines used for the conversion of mechanical energy to electrical current), thus gaining the ability to produce current in the amounts needed for various applications. He designed a system for delivering that current safely to houses and invented electrical lights, sockets, switches, meters, and fuses. Edison also built the manufacturing plants for all of the above. One of these early manufacturing plants became the General Electric Company.

On Monday, September 4, 1882, the lights came on in 85 New York City homes, ushering in the age of electricity. By 1886 more than 500 lighting plants were in operation, producing electricity for factories and other specific needs. Fifty-two U.S. cities had central power stations by then; electricity would not be brought to many rural areas until after World War II. Meanwhile electrical power systems were being installed in Europe, South America, and Japan. This time was productive and lucrative for Edison; he also continued his work on other inventions, applying for 141 patents in 1882 alone. His organization owned assets worth about $10 million early in the 1880s.

Labeled a genius by many, Edison often said that genius was "ninety-nine per cent perspiration and one per cent inspiration," and he himself worked long hours. Among his inventions are the mimeograph machine,

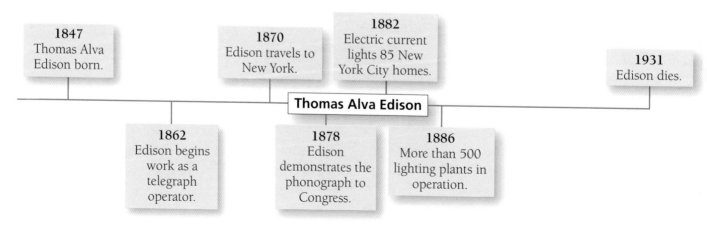

| 1847 Thomas Alva Edison born. | | 1870 Edison travels to New York. | 1882 Electric current lights 85 New York City homes. | | 1931 Edison dies. |

Thomas Alva Edison

| 1862 Edison begins work as a telegraph operator. | 1878 Edison demonstrates the phonograph to Congress. | 1886 More than 500 lighting plants in operation. |

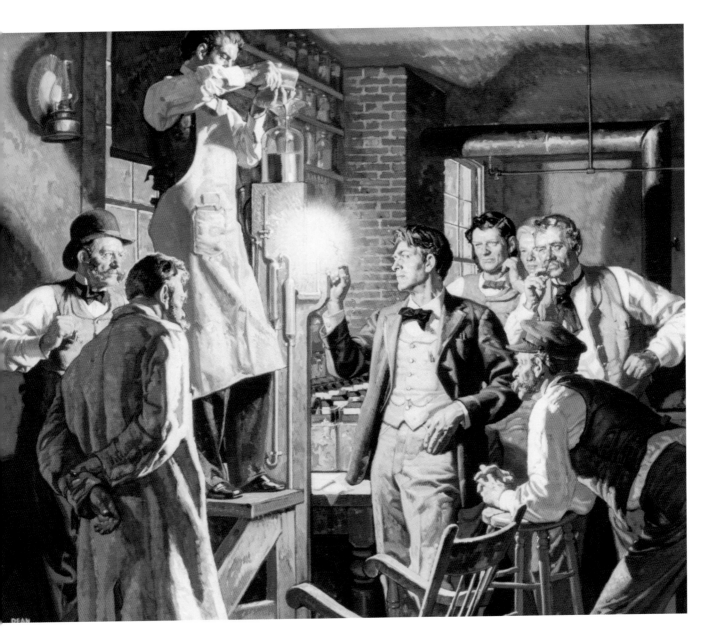

the rheostat, the microphone, the forerunner of the vacuum tube, the phonograph, the incandescent lamp, the magnetic ore separator, the motion picture camera, the fluoroscope, and the alkaline storage battery. He also developed improvements for devices invented by others, the telephone among them. He was granted more than 1,000 U.S. patents—more than any other single person.

When Edison died in 1931, it was proposed that the most fitting memorial would be for the president of the United States to order all electric current turned off for two minutes throughout the country. This did not happen, however, because only 50 years after Edison had brought his wire into a few homes for early trials, no one could imagine life without electricity, not even for two minutes.

An illustration of a young Edison (center, with lightbulb) and colleagues at his Menlo Park research lab.

Further Reading

Baldwin, Neil. *Edison: Inventing the Century.* Chicago: University of Chicago Press, 2001.

Edison, Thomas A. *The Diary and Sundry Observations of Thomas Alva Edison.* Edited by Dagobert D. Runes. New York: Greenwood Press, 1968.

Friedel, Robert D., and Paul Israel. *Edison's Electric Light: Biography of an Invention.* New Brunswick, N.J.: Rutgers University Press, 1986.

Israel, Paul. *Edison: A Life of Invention.* New York: John Wiley & Sons, 1998.

Josephson, Matthew. *Edison: A Biography.* New York: McGraw-Hill, 1959.

—*Gary Baughn*

See also:
Education Industry; National
Education Association.

Edison Schools, Inc.

Edison Schools, Inc., was not the first for-profit education management company in the United States, but it is probably the name most recognized in that field. However, more than a decade since its founding, Edison has yet to turn a profit and has achieved mixed results in two vital areas—financial health and student performance.

Chris Whittle, an innovative media entrepreneur from Tennessee, first envisioned what would eventually become the Edison Project in 1989, when he was asked to make a speech on improving public education. Whittle's idea was to start from scratch and have schools run like businesses, making them more efficient and performance-oriented. At the same time, the United States was grappling with President George H. W. Bush's proposals for education reform. (Indeed, Chester E. Finn, Jr., one of the main forces behind Bush's plan for school vouchers, became part of the Edison design team.) The time seemed ripe for innovation.

Initially, Whittle envisioned a network of 1,000 private schools educating nearly two million students nationwide. Tuition would be $5,500 per year—roughly, the equivalent of government expenditures for the education of each American child. The Edison Project anticipated opening 200 campuses by the 1996 school year, and, operating on a 15 percent profit margin, expected to earn revenues of nearly $700 million. Revenues were predicted to increase to more than $10 billion by the year 2000.

Several partners in Whittle's media empire, Whittle Communications, funded Edison's design stage, which began in 1991. Time Warner pledged 37.5 percent of the $40 million needed to develop the Edison Project (some estimates were as high as $60 million), and the balance was picked up by other investors. Whittle was able to secure such funds primarily because of his former successes, which, in the realm of education included the controversial and profitable Channel One, which Whittle founded in 1989. Channel One brought televisions and teen-oriented educational programming into classrooms, paid for in full by advertisers and corporate underwriters eager for a young, captive audience.

After four years of research and development, the plan for the Edison Project had changed drastically. President Bush failed to secure a national voucher system, which shrank Edison's potential market. Edison, in turn, could not secure the additional funding needed for its 1,000-school plan. In lieu of creating a network of private schools, the Edison Project came up with a new plan—to contract with school districts to manage existing public schools, functioning in a manner similar to that of Education Alternatives, Inc., the American pioneer in for-profit education. Edison believed it was poised to succeed because of a simple economic principle—economies of scale.

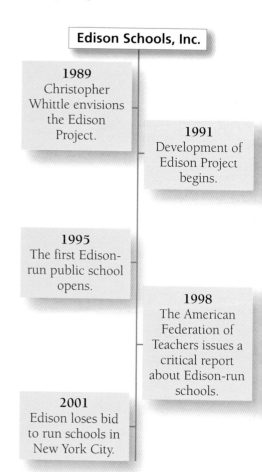

Edison Schools, Inc.

1989
Christopher Whittle envisions the Edison Project.

1991
Development of Edison Project begins.

1995
The first Edison-run public school opens.

1998
The American Federation of Teachers issues a critical report about Edison-run schools.

2001
Edison loses bid to run schools in New York City.

The average school district operates six schools; Edison sought to operate hundreds. Relying on a central body to consolidate and manage business affairs, Edison planned to pay for provided services and even make a profit by cutting operating costs in support services, including food service, transportation, and administration. For example, the Dodge-Edison school in Wichita, Kansas, had been paying $68,000 for payroll processing; Edison hired an outside contractor for $3,000. Edison's critics point to some cuts, such as the use of unsalaried and nonunion "intern" teachers, and raise questions about the effect of cost-cutting measures on children's education.

On August 1, 1995, the first Edison-run public school, George Washington Elementary, in Sherman, Texas, opened. The school attracted nearly 150 new students, which brought total enrollment to almost 500 that year. Within weeks, Edison schools were opened in Kansas, Michigan, and Massachusetts. By June 1996, at least one of Edison's schools boasted of a waiting list of more than 300. Many parents were attracted to Edison's extras: a longer school day, a longer school year, mandatory Spanish classes beginning in kindergarten, extracurricular activities like music classes, a computer in every classroom and one in every child's home. Regardless of the extras and promises of results-oriented teaching, others, including many esteemed educators, questioned the very foundation of a company whose bottom line was not necessarily children's education.

In May 1998, the American Federation of Teachers (AFT) issued a report about student achievement in Edison-run schools. Edison, then 25 schools strong, had boasted of raising test scores across the board; however, the AFT report showed inconclusive results and criticized Edison on several key points—high teacher turnover, use of inexperienced teachers, large class sizes, and failure to properly implement the "Success for All" reading program. In a similar report released in

Edison Schools founder Christopher Whittle in an undated photo.

October 2000, the AFT stated firmly that Edison's 40 schools were performing no better than comparable public schools.

In 2001, Edison's growth and prestige began to slip noticeably. The company lost an important bid to manage several public schools in the New York City area. Not only was this a professional blow, as Edison is headquartered in Manhattan, it also amounted to a huge loss in growth and, thus, potential profits. At roughly the same time, news of Edison's shaky relationship with the school district of San Francisco hit the papers, with San Francisco threatening to break its contract. In addition, the company, then a decade old, had yet to turn a profit.

By the end of 2001, Edison was poised to capitalize on an opportunity to manage dozens of troubled schools in Philadelphia. Pennsylvania governor Tom Ridge had indicated Edison as his choice; however, when Ridge left his governorship to head the federal Office of Homeland Security in late 2001, Edison lacked statewide political support. Extremely vocal public opposition further threatened the company's position. Then the Securities and Exchange

Odessa Watford, right, whose children attend Community School 66 in New York City, protests against the school becoming an Edison School. The Edison proposal was defeated.

Commission began to question Edison's accounting practices.

Edison ultimately took charge of a portion of Philadelphia's schools but lost several contracted schools, including seven in Dallas, lowering its total to just 135 schools throughout the country. To help pay for the Philadelphia schools, Edison scrapped plans to build a $125 million national headquarters and kindergarten in Harlem. By August 2002, Nasdaq threatened to delist Edison if it did not raise its stock price to $1 within 90 days. Edison's initial public offering, in November 1999, was 6.8 million shares at $18 a share. Soon after, Whittle put his $46 million private estate on the market, reportedly to defray personal losses caused by Edison's falling stock price.

Despite these setbacks, in September 2002 representatives of Edison suggested, perhaps optimistically, that the company could be profitable by 2004. Edison has had a significant voice in debate about American education, from reform to vouchers and charter schools, and has contributed to the national debate about for-profit education.

Further Reading

Edison Schools, Inc. *Fourth Annual Report of School Performance,* September 2001. http://www.edisonschools.com/annualreport2001 part1.pdf; http://www.edisonschools.com/ annualreport2001part2.pdf (January 8, 2003).

Nelson, F. Howard. *Trends in Student Achievement for Edison Schools, Inc.: The Emerging Track Record.* Washington, D.C.: American Federation of Teachers, 2000.

Ravitch, Diane, and Joseph Viteritti, eds. *New Schools for a New Century: The Redesign of Urban Education.* New Haven, Conn.: Yale University Press, 1997.

Trimble, Vance H. *The Empire Undone: The Wild Rise and Hard Fall of Chris Whittle.* Secaucus, N.J.: Carol Publishing Group, 1995.

—*Laura Lambert*

Education Industry

The term *industry* usually connotes a wide amalgamation of firms that are closely aligned in a common area of interest, as in the defense industry and the automobile industry. Until recently the term *education industry* was unnecessary, because the phrase "schools, colleges, and universities" sufficed. However, the late twentieth century saw the creation of newer education organizations that are distinct from traditional schools.

Because the education industry is so new and rapidly evolving, no widespread consensus has been reached on the businesses or even categories of businesses that make up the industry. In particular, many use the phrase "education industry" to refer only to the largely for-profit firms that have emerged relatively recently, while others also include the traditional public and nonprofit schools, colleges, and universities as part of the education industry. The more limited definition is used here.

Education Delivery Firms

The many firms, which tend to be small and serve specialized markets, that make up the education industry are not household names. Most fall into one of three major categories based on the market they serve. The biggest of these primary markets (more than 50 percent of the industry) is called pre-K–12, referring to the grade levels of the children who receive these services. Firms serving this market include those that provide child care, regular schooling for children in kindergarten through grade 12, and specialized schooling services for children who have special needs. Examples of pre-K–12 education delivery firms include KinderCare Learning Centers and Bright Horizons Family Solutions in the child care area, Edison Schools and Nobel Learning Centers in grades K–12, and Aspen Education Group and Ombudsman in specialty schools.

Another group of businesses provides services to employed adults working in corporations. Firms providing services in the corporate market enable working adults to go to school and upgrade their skills. Firms in the corporate market account for nearly 30 percent of total annual revenues of the education industry. Examples include Global Knowledge and Learning Tree. Although these firms provide schooling for adults, their programs differ from those of most colleges; these firms generally offer shorter, noncredit-granting courses of instruction, which may lead to certificates based on satisfactory completion.

The third primary market for firms in the education industry is the same as that of traditional colleges and universities. This postsecondary market is served by firms that provide traditional, credit-granting, semester-long courses leading to formal degrees: associate, bachelor's, and master's. This sector accounts for less than 20 percent of total annual revenues of the education industry. Examples of firms serving this market are Apollo Group, which provides higher education for working adults, and DeVry University, which offers classes and degrees in business and technology. Some education delivery firms are dedicated to

See also:
Edison Schools, Inc.;
Outsourcing; Privatization.

An illustration of a nineteenth-century one-room schoolhouse, from American Educational Monthly, *October 1873.*

delivering accredited distance education or e-learning; for example, the firm K12 serves elementary students, and Capella University and University of Phoenix Online both serve postsecondary students.

All of the examples above share one characteristic, regardless of differences in their primary market: Their core business is education delivery. They provide teaching services to students.

Content, Infrastructure, and Services Firms

In addition to the many firms in the education industry whose core business is education delivery, many other firms specialize in one of three other kinds of core businesses. Some firms specialize in content—for example, the curriculum that is to be learned and then tested. Firms whose core business is content focus primarily on publishing textbooks and other curriculum

materials and (especially in the pre-K–12 market) materials for testing student knowledge of the curriculum. Pearson Education, Thomson Learning, and McGraw Hill Education are examples of content firms. A relatively large fraction of publishing for the corporate training market is provided by firms specializing in electronic learning or e-learning. Firms in this area develop software-driven training programs that corporate employees use at computer terminals located near their place of employment.

Other firms specialize in infrastructure—the largely physical goods associated with teaching and learning. Infrastructure firms may sell computer hardware, networking equipment, software, and Web-based applications to schools and colleges as well as offering training programs in the use of technology. Blackboard, SkillSoft,

A junior at Lowell High School in San Francisco looks at a brochure about the SAT tests at a Kaplan Learning Center. She is taking prep courses for the SAT.

Some education delivery firms specialize in continuing education for adults.

Plato, and Renaissance Learning are examples of education infrastructure firms. Others are, in effect, education divisions of larger, noneducation firms, Microsoft for instance. Still other firms may manufacture and distribute a variety of products, equipment, supplies, and curriculum materials to schools and colleges.

Finally, a relatively small number of firms in the education industry specialize in the core business of educational services. Educational services firms provide tutoring, test preparation services, testing and assessment, and other forms of professional development. Examples include Sylvan Learning, Kaplan, and Princeton Review. The SAT and ACT examinations for college entrance and the GMAT, GRE, and LSAT exams for graduate schools are produced by educational services firms.

Trends in the Education Industry

Traditional schools, colleges, and universities are often characterized as comprehensive (offering many services to many different kinds of students). The newer education businesses are much more specialized in the goods and services they offer. Most of these newer firms did not exist a generation ago. What prompted the creation and growth of these companies? Greater reliance on private for-profit businesses to provide education—often referred to as the privatization of education—

provides a description of but not an explanation for this change. Five interacting trends since the 1980s have together fostered privatization in education.

New Sources of Revenue. Limits on tax revenues for funding public institutions have encouraged education leaders to pursue new or nontraditional revenue sources. Among these new sources are tax appropriations to programs other than education but related to it: for example, juvenile justice, health, early childhood development. Other sources include donations from nonprofit education philanthropists and "donations" from businesses in exchange for advertising or even access to student markets, and investments from for-profit education businesses. As the relative share of nontax revenues for education has grown, so too has the share of nongovernment-run educational businesses.

Greater Reliance on Outsourcing. Rather than providing goods and services within a school or college, educators are contracting with specialty firms to provide a better good or service at a better price because they specialize. These specialty firms—public, nonprofit, and for-profit organizations—provide direct services to students via contracts with public education organizations or charge fees directly to students. Specialties range from music lessons to technology training to teaching services for children with learning disabilities.

Increasing Competition. Traditional geographic segmentation of education services—what school one attends being determined solely by where one lives—is giving way to competition across these old boundaries. Since the 1980s, charter schools, magnet schools, voucher programs, interdistrict transfer, and open enrollment policies have grown up alongside the fixed-attendance boundaries of neighborhood public schools. Distance-education and home-schooling programs are delivered across state boundaries as well as across boundaries of regional accrediting agencies. As these political barriers-to-entry fall, new "virtual" education businesses providing online education, like K12 and Capella University, are increasingly able to serve students across attendance area, district, state, and national boundaries.

Increasing Emphasis on Performance. In K–12 and community college systems especially, state governments are increasingly tying state funding to student academic performance while relaxing laws that require compliance with uniform procedures. California, for example, now provides financial rewards to schools that exceed their performance targets and intervenes in schools that are under-performing. Schools can request waivers from regulations governing how they must operate. As a consequence of these changes, new education businesses (and new programs created by existing education businesses) that promise higher student performance are more acceptable in the market than they had been.

Increasing Reliance on Technology. Rapid developments in technology are enabling

Careers in the Education Industry

The primary occupation of those in the education industry is that of teacher. Within the teaching field, various levels of professional training are necessary. Some adult education centers, for example, those teaching English as a second language or preparing students for the G.E.D., may require only that the teachers complete a training course. Teachers in the public schools are generally required to have an undergraduate degree in education or a related field, and most U.S. states require additional certification and training.

Blending education with business has led to the creation of a vast number of employment opportunities beyond the realm of teaching. For example, the Scholastic Aptitude Test (SAT) has engendered a mini-industry of its own, from preparing students to take the exam to grading the results. Education delivery firms also require curriculum specialists to actually create the programs of study used in the classrooms. Publishers are needed to produce the necessary textbooks and educational materials. As many resources are available online, educational institutions and delivery firms employ technology specialists to produce the necessary software used in online teaching.

Many education delivery firms serving both adolescents and adults are for-profit organizations. Thus, they require personnel who are able to manage the financial and business aspects of the firm, while also understanding the unique challenges presented by an education environment. Though the education industry does not offer the most remunerative careers, many in the field believe it to be among the most rewarding. Job prospects in the education industry are bright, as a large proportion of teachers will be retiring while the population continues to increase.

—*Colleen Sullivan*

Content development and education infrastructure firms provide educational tools, like textbooks and software.

the creation of new education businesses, fundamentally altering the organization and service mix and reach of many education organizations. A number of new education firms have emerged whose core mission entails some form of e-learning; Riverdeep, K12, Cisco, and WebCT are examples.

Issues in the Education Industry

Education has no shortage of contentious issues, in large part because education is very visible and many people feel they have a stake in it. Education affects the daily lives of more people than virtually any other industry. Decisions about schooling are quite decentralized in the United States, with separate bodies presiding over (and arguing about) 50 state college systems, 50 community college systems, some 15,000 school districts, and more than 100,000 public and private

schools. Consequently, many issues in education continually surface and are widely debated. Many of these issues involve differences of opinion about the right answers to one or more of three broad questions: Who should pay for education and how much? Who should provide education? and Who should receive education and what kind?

These long-standing questions are being increasingly debated with specific reference to the education industry, especially with reference to the pre-K–12 and the postsecondary markets. The central issue is often framed as one of privatization, because the long-standing dominance of government (public) financing and provision of education are being eroded by new, private for-profit organizations.

Opponents of some forms of privatization fear that private firms will be less

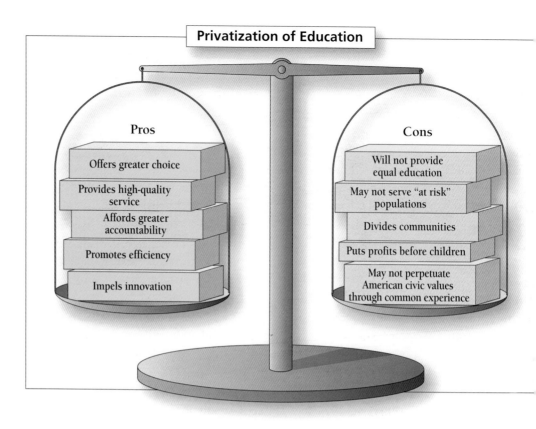

Privatization of Education

Pros
- Offers greater choice
- Provides high-quality service
- Affords greater accountability
- Promotes efficiency
- Impels innovation

Cons
- Will not provide equal education
- May not serve "at risk" populations
- Divides communities
- Puts profits before children
- May not perpetuate American civic values through common experience

concerned with equality of access to education than governments have been. They also fear that with privatization comes greater choice, which could leave some families at a disadvantage. Some critics have philosophical problems with school choice. The fundamental premise of American education has been that every American has the right to an equal education: to foster choice is to support the presumption that some schools are, in fact, better than others. Finally, many opposed to privatization maintain that profit should not be a factor in the education of children.

Proponents of some forms of privatization, on the other hand, argue that with it and school choice, students least well served by the current public system will have better schools than would otherwise be the case. In addition, they contend that for-profit firms are likely to be more efficient and to innovate more aggressively. In this view, the profit motive is an inducement to provide high-quality services because the schools and firms must compete to get and retain their customers, that is, students and their parents.

Further fueling the debate about privatization has been the entry of industrialized countries into the information age or knowledge economy. More than ever, what individuals know and can do determines their personal lifetime earnings as well as the overall economic well-being of their communities. Accordingly the demands for schooling have been pushed to a level that is very difficult for governments alone to supply.

Further Reading

Boyles, Deron. *American Education and Corporations.* New York: Garland, 1998.

Carnoy, Martin, ed. *International Encyclopedia of Economics of Education.* New York: Elsevier Science, 2000.

Etzkovitz, Henry, and Loet Leydesdorff, eds. *Universities and the Global Knowledge Economy.* New York: Continuum International Publishing, 2002.

Kohn, Alfie, and Patrick Shannon, eds. *Education, Inc.: Turning Learning into a Business.* Westport, Conn.: Heinemann, 2002.

Witte, John F., Jr. *The Market Approach to Education: An Analysis of America's First Voucher Program.* Princeton, N.J.: Princeton University Press, 1999.

—*Guilbert C. Hentschke*

E-Mail

Few innovations throughout history have fundamentally transformed society by changing the way people communicate with each other. The most recent of these innovations is e-mail. E-mail has changed the way we communicate, the way we do business, even the way we speak to each other. As with other innovations, however, e-mail has come with its own set of limitations and problems.

Inventing E-mail

Although we now associate e-mail with the Internet, e-mail actually predates the Web. In 1968 the United States Defense Department began to build ARPANET, the precursor to the Internet. One of the companies hired to develop ARPANET was Bolt, Beranek, and Newman (BBN). In 1971 Ray Tomlinson, an engineer working for BBN, wrote a program called SNDMSG, which allowed programmers and researchers who were working on Digital PDP-10s—one of the early ARPANET computers—to leave messages for each other. This program was similar to others already in existence—it allowed the exchange of messages between users who shared the same machine. Users could create a text file and deliver it to a mailbox. SNDMSG allowed users to write more material onto the end of the mailbox, but it could not send or receive messages from other computers.

At that time, ARPANET had been installed at 15 universities and companies around the country. To transfer files between computers located at different ARPANET nodes, Tomlinson created a second program, called CYPNET.

In 1972 Tomlinson adapted CYPNET to use SNDMSG to deliver messages to mailboxes on remote machines through the ARPANET. Tomlinson chose the @ symbol to distinguish between messages addressed to mailboxes on local computers and messages that were headed out onto the network. Using two PDP-10 computers in his office, which were connected together only by ARPANET, Tomlinson sent himself an e-mail message—the world's first. What was this first, groundbreaking message? When asked, Tomlinson could not remember exactly, but he thought it was QWERTYUIOP or a similar string of letters.

Tomlinson next sent a message to his ARPANET colleagues, letting them know about the new message system. Before long, the various ARPANET groups were using e-mail for almost all communications. So successful did e-mail become that within a few years, the development of e-mail protocols had almost taken over as the primary function of the ARPANET.

In 1974 ARPANET researchers Vinton Cerf and Bob Kahn published "A Protocol for Packet Network Intercommunication," which specified the design of a Transmission Control Program (TCP) that could send messages rapidly in discrete packets. The paper also introduced the idea of gateways, where

See also:
E-Business; Information Technology; Internet; Telecommunications Industry.

How E-mail Works

As a business and communication tool, e-mail is invaluable. Like all tools, to get the most out of it, it is useful to know how it works.

E-MAIL CLIENTS

The e-mail client is the program that lets you look at your e-mail. There are stand-alone clients like Microsoft Outlook, Outlook Express, Eudora, or Pegasus programs; clients attached to Web pages like Hotmail and Yahoo; and Internet service providers, for example, America Online, that have their own e-mail clients.

E-MAIL SERVERS

E-mail requires a server for the client to connect to. Servers are programs that run all the time on huge computers. For most people, the e-mail system consists of two different servers. One is the Simple Mail Transfer Protocol (SMTP) Server, which handles outgoing mail. The other is the Post Office Protocol (POP) Server, which handles incoming mail.

Each e-mail server maintains a text file (account) for each person who can receive e-mail. Server programs "listen" to specific ports, waiting for people or programs to attach to the port.

When the writer clicks on the Send icon, the e-mail client connects to the server and sends the server the address and the message. The server then formats that information and adds it to the receiver's account. The account accumulates until the receiver's e-mail client connects to the server machine and collects the messages.

ATTACHMENTS

E-mail messages can contain only text information, but many attachments are not text and require processing through a program called uuencode. The uuencode program converts the original file into an encoded version that contains only text characters. In the early days of e-mail, senders would run uuencode, then paste the uuencoded file into their e-mail message. The recipient would then run a program called uudecode to translate it. E-mail clients now run uuencode and uudecode automatically.

only the receiver can read the contents of messages. That same year, BBN released Telenet, the first commercial version of ARPANET. Along with Telenet, of course, came e-mail capability.

Throughout the 1970s, ARPANET continued to expand and grow as new protocols were developed that made the network easier to use. Soon new networks, not connected to ARPANET and the U.S. Defense Department, began to spring up. These early networks included CSNET (Computer and Science Network), BITNET (Because It's Time Network), EUNet (European UNIX Network), and USENET (User Group Network).

Emoticons

Because vocal inflections and facial expressions are absent from e-mail and other online communication, sometimes other clues have to be added to avoid misunderstandings. Emoticons are combinations of keyboard characters used in communications between computer users to provide information about the writer's feelings and state of mind; they are online emotion. Many emoticons depict facial expressions and are also called smileys. Western emoticons are usually interpreted sideways—the page has to be turned mentally 90 degrees clockwise. Japanese emoticons, by contrast, do not have to be rotated.

The invention of the smiley is usually credited to Scott Fahlman who used one in a posting to the bulletin board system at Carnegie Mellon University around 1980. He later wrote: "I wish I had saved the original post, or at least recorded the date for posterity, but I had no idea that I was starting something that would soon pollute all the world's communication channels." From that original posting a seemingly never-ending flow of emoticons has arisen.

Emoticons have long been controversial among Internet users. Many purists resent their cute nature and argue that one's words should speak for themselves. Preferred in some circles are Internet acronyms such as LOL for "Laughing Out Loud" and HTH for "Hope This Helps."

—*Raúl Rojas*

EMOTICONS: A PARTIAL LIST

Western Emoticons

:-)	Smiley
:-(	Unhappy
;-)	Winking
;-(	Crying
:-0	Yelling
:-/	Skeptical
:-o	Surprise
:-#	Censored
:-*	Kiss
:——}	You lie like Pinocchio
:?)	Philosopher
@(_)~~~	Hot coffee
:-)(-:	Just married!
:-)x===>	A tie

Japanese Emoticons

(^_^)	Ear-to-ear smile
*^_^*	Blushing smile
(^.^)/	User is waving hello
__m_oo_m__	Spying over the wall
m(_ _)m	Deep bow used for apologizing or expressing thanks
>——(^_^)——<	A hug

ACRONYMS

<G>	Grinning		BTW	By the way
LOL	Laughing out loud		YMMV	Your mileage may vary
ROFL	Rolling on the floor laughing		OIC	Oh, I see
TIC	Tongue in cheek		HTH	Hope this helps
IMHO	In my humble opinion		AFK	Away from keyboard
IMNSHO	In my not so humble opinion		BFN	Bye for now
FWIW	For what it's worth			

E-mail in Business

The advantages of e-mail were obvious from the beginning. In a paper published in 1978 by the Institute of Electrical and Electronic Engineers, two important figures in the creation of the ARPANET, J. C. R. Licklider and Albert Vezza, explained the popularity of e-mail. "One of the advantages of the message systems over letter mail was that, in an ARPANET message, one could write tersely and type imperfectly, even to an older person in a superior position and even to a person one did not know very well, and the recipient took no offense. . . . one could proceed immediately to the point without having to engage in small talk first . . . the message services produced a preservable record . . . the sender and receiver did not have to be available at the same time." Licklider and Vezza had foreseen many of the aspects of e-mail that make it an invaluable tool for businesses today.

E-mail has greatly increased the pace of business. Reports and documents can be sent overseas immediately; a message sent at night in one time zone will be waiting when the recipient gets into the office—no need for late-night phone calls; and small talk can be dispensed with. In countries where the government controls the official media, e-mail often provides an alternative, informal communications network.

In June 2000 the Electronic Signatures in Global and National Commerce Act became law. This bill recognizes e-signatures as legal and made possible the conducting of many more kinds of business via e-mail.

Security Concerns

E-mail communication is not more secure than other forms of communication. E-mails transmitted via company electronic mail systems are legally considered company property and not private communication. Unlike postal mail, which no one but the addressee may legally read (without a government warrant), all e-mail sent at work may be reviewed or monitored at any time by an employer. Clicking on delete removes your selected e-mail messages only from your personal mail; a copy still exists on the company server.

Messages sent from home may also not be private. E-mail may remain on the Internet service provider's server, or in a backup, for several months. Any skilled technician can recover the e-mail message's "ghost" from the networked system. Although such retrieval has been a great help in investigating crimes, it can be used unscrupulously.

Spam, or junk e-mail, is an even worse problem than postal junk mail. Spammers harvest e-mail addresses from chat rooms and other messaging systems by intercepting Internet traffic and analyzing it for strings of characters that resemble an e-mail address. A computer connected to the Internet can distribute thousands of messages an hour at virtually no cost to the advertiser. Spammed messages and ads are also a favorite place to hide computer viruses, which cause millions of dollars of damage to computers every year.

Protection

E-mail can be made more secure by using encryption. One popular encryption program is PGP, which stands for Pretty Good Privacy. This permits the user to select the length of the code that is used to encrypt and authenticate messages. Many businesses also use perimeter defense devices called firewalls. The firewall is an intermediate computer that passes data back and forth between the Internet and the company network. The firewall computer can be programmed to pass only virus-free e-mail, or only e-mail from business partners, and block anything else (for example, spam or personal mail) from coming in or out.

For the greatest protection from virus attacks, businesses now use e-mail without any connection between their network and the Internet. Many small firms simply have

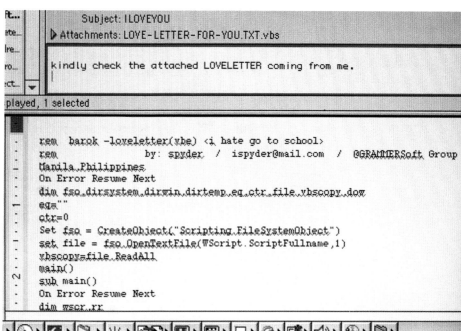

their employees check their e-mail by dialing out with a modem to reach the Internet service provider. The employees' own computers, and other computers in the firm's network, are thus almost completely protected from outside attack. Russia was not attacked by the 2000 ILOVEYOU virus because Russia's major computer networks had not yet been connected to the Internet.

Despite problems, e-mail has become an integral part of the communications landscape. Even people who grew up with "snail" mail and the telephone are wondering how they ever got along without e-mail.

The text of the ILOVEYOU virus as it appeared in an e-mail in Hong Kong.

Further Reading

Civin, Michael A. *Male, Female, Email: The Struggle for Relatedness in a Paranoid Society.* New York: Other Press, 1999.

Gurian, Phil. *E-mail Business Strategies & Dozens of Other Great Ways to Take Advantage of the Internet.* Spokane, Wash.: Grand National Press, 2002.

Miller, Joan E. *Yada, Yada, Yada.Com.Org.Edu.Gov.Email: What I Learned on the www/Internet—Total Nonsense.* New York: Lightning Source Publishing, 2000.

Mulligan, Geoff. *Removing the Spam: Email Processing and Filtering.* Reading, Mass.: Addison-Wesley Publishing, 1999.

Tunstall, Joan. *Better, Faster Email: Getting the Most Out of Email.* New York: Allen & Unwin, 1999.

—Lisa Magloff

Energy Industry

Energy creates the capacity to perform work. It is the master resource for the modern world, enabling people to gather, transport, and transform natural resources into useful products for longer, more comfortable, and more productive lives. The crucial role of energy explains the prominent place of the energy industry in the United States and the world.

History of the Energy Industry

Throughout most of human history, energy was the work of human muscle powered by the calories in food. Then between eight and 10 thousand years ago, domesticated cattle, horses, and donkeys lent their muscle to humanity's struggle for survival and progress. This animate energy era was followed by the renewable energy era, in which people used wind to power sailing vessels, falling water to turn gears and grinding mechanisms, and combustible plants and wood (biomass) to provide light and heat for warmth and cooking. These energy sources seemed inexhaustible and free, but they were not sufficiently concentrated, transportable, or reliable to fuel an industrial society.

In the mid-sixteenth century, a wood shortage in England caused timber prices to rise. The resulting switch to coal for fuel marked the onset of the hydrocarbon age. By

U.S. Energy Time Line

Mid-Sixteenth Century
Hydrocarbon age begins as England switches from wood to coal.

Mid-Nineteenth Century
Coal oil, coal gas, and crude oil first used for fuel.

1878
First U.S. hydroelectric power plant completed.

1882
Thomas Edison opens first electricity-generating plant.

1904
Electricity first produced from geothermal steam.

1929
First use of pumped hydropower.

1956
First commercial nuclear reactor completed.

1966
First tidal power plant opened.

Early 1980s
Large wind farms begin to be developed.

1983
First solar electric generating system built.

1996
First use of commercial fuel cell run on renewable fuel.

						Renewable Energy			
U.S. Energy Production 1960 to 1999 (in quadrillion British thermal units [BTUs])									
Year	Crude oil	Natural gas	Coal	Nuclear power	Total[1]	Hydro-electric power	Biofuel[2]	Solar	Total[1]
1960	14.93	12.66	10.82	(Z)	41.49	1.61	1.32	(-)	2.93
1965	16.52	15.78	13.06	(Z)	49.34	2.06	1.34	(-)	3.40
1970	20.40	21.67	14.61	0.24	63.50	2.63	1.43	(-)	4.07
1975	17.73	19.64	14.99	1.90	61.36	3.16	1.50	(-)	4.72
1980	18.25	19.91	18.60	2.74	67.24	2.90	2.48	(-)	5.49
1985	18.99	16.98	19.33	4.15	67.72	2.97	2.86	(-)	6.03
1990	15.57	18.36	22.46	6.16	70.85	3.05	2.67	0.06	6.16
1991	15.70	18.23	21.59	6.58	67.51	3.02	2.68	0.07	6.15
1992	15.22	18.38	21.63	6.61	70.06	2.62	2.83	0.07	5.90
1993	14.49	18.58	20.25	6.52	68.37	2.89	2.78	0.07	6.15
1994	14.10	9.35	22.11	6.84	70.83	2.69	2.91	0.07	6.08
1995	13.89	19.10	22.03	7.18	71.29	3.21	3.04	0.07	6.68
1996	13.72	19.36	22.68	7.17	72.58	3.59	3.10	0.08	7.15
1997	13.66	19.39	23.21	6.68	72.53	3.72	2.98	0.07	7.14
1998	13.24	19.29	23.72	7.16	72.55	3.35	2.99	0.07	6.78
1999	12.54	19.30	23.33	7.73	72.52	3.23	3.51	0.08	7.18

(Z) = fewer than 50 trillion. (-) = or rounds to zero. [1] Includes types not shown separately. [2] Includes wood, wood waste, peat, wood liquors, railroad ties, pitch, wood sludge, municipal solid waste, agricultural waste, straw, tires, landfill gases, fish oils, and other waste.
Source: U.S. Energy Information Administration, *Annual Energy Review, 2000*, Washington, D.C., Government Printing Office, 2000.

the mid-nineteenth century, coal was joined by coal oil, coal gas, and crude oil. Natural gas followed. These primary energy sources were concentrated, convenient, and easily transportable. They powered machines and vehicles and were later used to produce that most versatile and convenient form of energy—electricity.

In the mid-twentieth century, nuclear power also was harnessed to produce electricity. Experimentation continued after an energy crisis in the 1970s spawned new interest in high-tech versions of the traditional renewable energy sources like biomass (ethanol and biodiesel fuels for transportation), wind (turbines to drive electric generators), solar (photovoltaics, that is, solar cells), and water (hydroelectric dams).

The Modern Energy Industry

Three petroleum products—gasoline, diesel, and aviation fuel—power nearly all forms of modern transportation. Fuel oil and natural gas dominate the heating market, while electricity dominates the lighting, air conditioning, and appliance markets. Electricity's share of the

Careers in the Energy Industry

Although a college degree is not a requirement for entry-level energy jobs, employers generally seek applicants with an aptitude for science, mathematics, or mechanics. However, more advanced and better paying jobs in the energy industry may require a considerable amount of study. Plant operators and technicians are required to take several training courses to acquire necessary certification, while engineers need advanced degree in their subspecialty. Although many jobs within the energy industry are not physically strenuous, some require workers to work one of three eight-hour shifts on a rotating basis. Such rotating shifts can cause disruptions in sleep patterns, and many people find them stressful. Certain occupations within the energy industry can be quite hazardous and require a great deal of physical strength, especially those of oil or natural gas field-worker. Such year-round outdoor jobs are done in all kinds of weather, exposing such workers to additional danger and stress.

The energy industry in the United States is likely to show limited growth in the near future. The country has few unexplored petroleum and natural gas resources, while public suspicion about the safety of nuclear power makes the construction of new nuclear plants or expansion of old ones unlikely. However, the technical skills acquired by energy workers can often lead to employment in other nations where the industry is not as developed.

—*Colleen Sullivan*

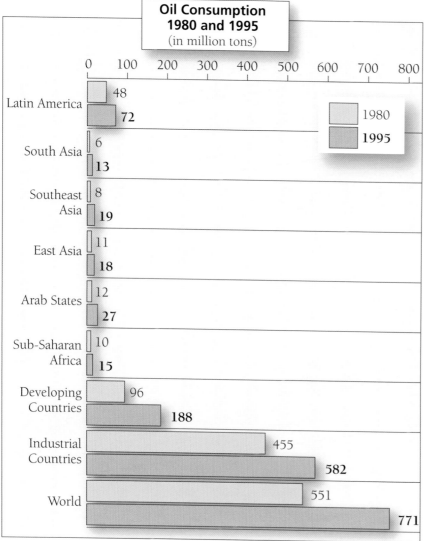

Oil Consumption 1980 and 1995
(in million tons)

Region	1980	1995
Latin America	48	72
South Asia	6	13
Southeast Asia	8	19
East Asia	11	18
Arab States	12	27
Sub-Saharan Africa	10	15
Developing Countries	96	188
Industrial Countries	455	582
World	551	771

Source: Global Policy Forum, *Social/Economic Policy,* http://www.globalpolicy.org/socecon/tables/oiluse1.htm (January 9, 2003).

energy market continues to expand as new uses for power are found.

Global revenues from the oil and natural gas industry (exploration, production, transportation, refining, and retailing) total about $2 trillion each year. However, oil and gas is a $5 trillion industry if related construction (for example, refineries and retail gas stations) and manufacturing (like oil field equipment) revenues are included. This amount is approximately equal to the entire U.S. economy. Exxon Mobil is the world's largest corporation, and Royal Dutch/Shell Group and BP are both in the top 10. Energy-dependent automobile and electronic companies populate the upper tier of global industrial concerns as well.

The largest energy firms are integrated to include exploration, production, transportation, and distribution activities. Oil "majors"—Exxon Mobil, Shell, and BP—produce, refine, and transport oil products and market them to motorists and other end users. The advantages of integration include internalized profit centers, standardized quality control procedures, locked-in sources and markets for each industry segment, and balanced risk between the upstream (exploration and production) and downstream (refining and marketing) segments. For example, profits lost in exploration and production because of low crude oil prices may be offset by increased profitability in refining and marketing—and vice versa. Overall, however, higher oil prices improve the profitability of integrated companies.

Integration has disadvantages. For example, while profits in one business segment may offset losses caused by market conditions in another, they may also mask losses caused by inefficiency and mismanagement. In addition, the sheer size of the major companies can make them less able to respond quickly to new opportunities and changing conditions.

These disadvantages have enabled nonintegrated independent companies to compete successfully against integrated companies in each area of the oil industry. Such success requires seizing opportunities that larger and better-capitalized rivals could not or would not exploit. Regulatory and tax advantages have also expanded the so-called competitive space for independents in relation to the majors. On the other hand, some independents have partly integrated to create new competitive niches for themselves—for example, oil producers that own pipelines and oil refiners that own service stations.

Natural gas companies, including oil majors involved in the gas industry, once tended toward integration, but government intervention beginning in the 1930s led firms to separate into exploration and production, transmission, and distribution companies. Electric utilities have traditionally been integrated into generation and distribution, but regulatory reforms that began in the 1970s have encouraged independent power producers and independent marketers to compete with franchised monopolists. Independent electricity transmission companies have not yet emerged, but changes in federal regulations may help to create a new, nonintegrated electricity segment in the industry.

Physical and Intellectual Capital

Energy is at its base a physical business. Concrete and steel in innumerable configurations are needed to produce, refine, and transport energy to market, but intellectual capital drives these physical assets. New ideas improve the operation of existing facilities and put new equipment into play. This entrepreneurial component of the energy business explains why these depletable resources (oil, gas, and coal) have grown more abundant—and less polluting—even as consumption has dramatically increased.

The world's proved reserves of crude oil are 15 times greater now than they were in the 1950s. World natural gas reserves are five times greater than they were in the mid-1960s. Coal reserves are four times greater than originally estimated in the 1950s and twice as great as all the known oil and gas reserves combined on an energy-equivalent basis. This expansion of depletable resources is explained by the human ingenuity and financial capital used to discover and develop new energy reserves. Such expansion also provides a counterargument to the pessimistic view that limited energy supplies will constrain economic growth in the near future. Nevertheless, both expanded supplies and improved efficiencies will be needed to meet the energy needs of a world population that is expected to reach nine billion by the middle of the twenty-first century.

Drilling for natural gas in the Gulf of Mexico.

Computers and the Internet play vital roles in virtually all facets of the energy industry. Most energy products are traded as commodities (generic, unbranded products like farm produce or raw materials). Spot oil, oil that is traded within a 30-day period rather than locked in under longer-term contracts, became actively traded for the first time in the 1970s. Natural gas and electricity commodification followed in the 1980s and 1990s, respectively. The telephone and fax machine were once the primary tools of the trader, but now most of the world's energy is traded online at the click of a mouse.

Public Policy

Because of the energy industry's economic importance, it has long attracted government attention. Outside the United States, most of the world's hydrocarbon resources are government owned. Some of the world's largest energy concerns, including Gazprom in Russia and Pemex in Mexico, are state owned. Even in the United States, natural gas and electrical power distribution are regulated as public utilities. A global trend toward privatization since the 1980s has reduced government ownership of energy assets, but energy socialism is still significant in Latin America, Africa, the Middle East, and elsewhere.

Sustainable energy is a key global policy issue. Although technology and regulation have overcome many problems of depletion and pollution, global warming associated with the combustion of hydrocarbons has become a major environmental issue. Critics of today's energy economy cite anthropogenic (human-made) climate change as the major reason why the hydrocarbon energy age must soon come to a close. They warn of major temperature increases, more extreme weather events, and unfavorable climatic surprises resulting from the greenhouse gases emitted when oil, gas, and particularly coal, are burned.

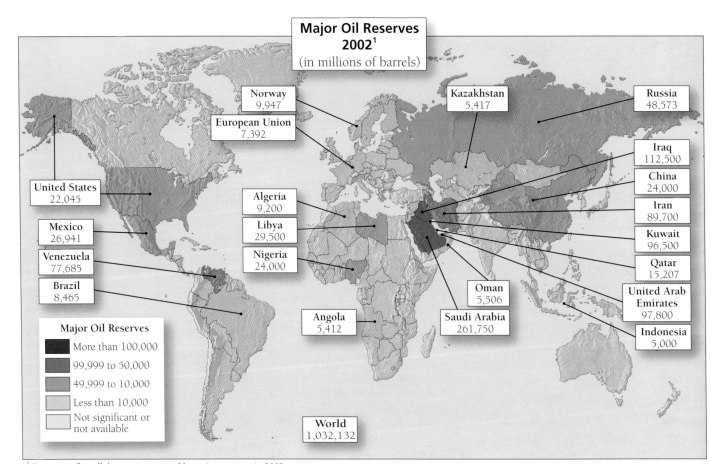

Major Oil Reserves 2002[1]
(in millions of barrels)

Norway 9,947
European Union 7,392
Kazakhstan 5,417
Russia 48,573
United States 22,045
Algeria 9,200
Iraq 112,500
China 24,000
Iran 89,700
Mexico 26,941
Libya 29,500
Kuwait 96,500
Venezuela 77,685
Nigeria 24,000
Qatar 15,207
Brazil 8,465
Oman 5,506
United Arab Emirates 97,800
Angola 5,412
Saudi Arabia 261,750
Indonesia 5,000
World 1,032,132

Major Oil Reserves
- More than 100,000
- 99,999 to 50,000
- 49,999 to 10,000
- Less than 10,000
- Not significant or not available

[1] Does not reflect all discoveries reported by various sources in 2002.
Source: Central Intelligence Agency, *CIA Factbook,* Washington, D.C., Government Printing Office, 2002.

A windmill farm generates power in the desert near Palm Springs, California.

Proponents of hydrocarbon energy call into question what they call climate alarmism. They point to the erratic nature, and thus supply, of wind- and solar-driven power generation and the difficulty of siting renewable energy projects (hydropower, wind, and geothermal) so that they do not create new, objectionable environmental effects.

Energy demand is expected to grow significantly in the decades ahead even as energy continues to be used more efficiently. A quarter of the world's population (1.6 billion people) has no access to electricity and other forms of modern energy. Great quantities of petroleum and electricity will be required as developing nations, including India and China, industrialize further. Technological advances continue to increase the demand for electricity in the developed world. The world's largest industry will continue to grow as demand increases for the "master resource."

Further Reading

Bradley, Robert. *Oil, Gas & Government: The U.S. Experience.* Lanham, Md.: Rowman & Littlefield, 1996.

Economides, Michael, and Ronald Oligney. *The Color of Oil.* Katy, Tex.: Round Oak, 2000.

Flavin, Christopher, and Nicholas Lenssen. *Power Surge: Guide to the Coming Energy Revolution.* New York: W. W. Norton, 1994.

Lomborg, Bjorn. *The Skeptical Environmentalist: Measuring the True State of the World.* Cambridge: Cambridge University Press, 2001.

Yergin, Daniel. *The Prize: The Epic Quest for Oil, Money, and Power.* New York: Simon & Schuster, 1991.

—*Robert Bradley*

See also:

Bankruptcy; Corporate Governance; Energy Industry.

Enron

The story of Enron Corporation is one of the most enigmatic and spectacular in business history. Enron was created by a series of acquisitions and mergers; the company's leadership team, led by Kenneth L. Lay, developed the first "coast to coast, border-to-border" natural gas pipeline system in the United States. The company also owned an exploration and production affiliate, a natural gas liquids business, an oil trading business, and a new natural gas marketing subsidiary.

From this base, Enron grew to become the largest wholesaler of natural gas and electricity in the United States and then Europe. The company also started ambitious new trading businesses in various commodities including water and broadband (high-speed Internet). It built pipelines and power plants around the world and embraced the Internet for its far-flung commodity marketing operation, calling itself a "new economy" company.

Enron's apparent successes attracted much praise. A *Fortune* magazine poll, for example, named Enron as America's most innovative company for six straight years. Lay, presiding over Enron's rise, became a leading figure in the energy industry and was considered the top entrepreneur of his generation. Some considered Lay to be in a league with the legendary Jack Welch of General Electric. Yet, in 2001, in a matter of weeks, Enron fell into bankruptcy and scandal. In the process, Lay's four-decade energy career, despite its many successes and innovations, was destroyed.

New Energy Visions
In late 1984 the *New York Times* profiled Ken Lay as "the maverick who transformed an industry." As president of Transco Energy Company, a natural gas production and interstate transmission company, Lay understood the new opportunities afforded by the partial deregulation of the natural gas industry. He reformed standard contracts between producers and pipelines to better align supply and demand. In the process, some of the first spot markets (30 days or less) for natural gas were created. However, Lay's real fame came after he left Transco and transformed a Texas-based natural gas pipeline company, Houston Natural Gas, into a multinational energy services giant, Enron.

Enron's competitive niche was formed by a transformation in public utility regulation. Traditionally, interstate natural gas pipelines sold the physical product and the transportation "bundled" together at a regulated price. Under the new open access requirements, interstate pipelines offered "unbundled" transportation services only and stopped buying and selling natural gas, which was not a profit center. Almost overnight, a vast new unregulated merchant business, natural gas marketing, was created in the interstate market.

Enron embraced the new world on both the business and regulatory fronts. Its interstate pipelines were the first to leave the merchant business in the late 1980s and early 1990s. The company lobbied for specific rules to help its marketing arm

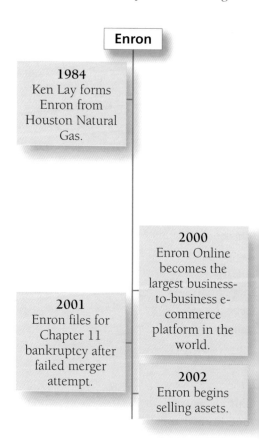

Enron

1984
Ken Lay forms Enron from Houston Natural Gas.

2000
Enron Online becomes the largest business-to-business e-commerce platform in the world.

2001
Enron files for Chapter 11 bankruptcy after failed merger attempt.

2002
Enron begins selling assets.

obtain nondiscriminatory access to all of the interstate pipelines in the United States. Enron quickly created a "first mover" advantage in the wholesale natural gas market, something that it would export to Europe and later recreate with electricity at home and abroad.

Enron and other companies like Dynegy developed a variety of risk management energy products in the new competitive arena for management of customer supply and price uncertainty. A customer could lock in a price for a month or years. Supply packages could be bought and delivered in specific geographic locations in a future year. These choices were greatly expanded from the plain offerings of the pipeline merchant era.

The new energy marketers worked by telephone and fax machine and in front of their computer screens. When the Internet came, it brought with it another revolution; by 2000 EnronOnline had become the largest business-to-business e-commerce platform in the world. More than $1 billion of online energy deals were consummated daily with Enron as the market maker. EnronOnline's reported revenues made Enron the seventh largest company in the United States in 2001.

Enron at its peak had two prize core businesses: a steadily profitable interstate natural gas pipeline division and a wholesale gas and power marketing operation. From this base, Enron forged into new areas. The company built power plants at home and abroad, including the world's largest natural-gas-fueled combined cycle plant, the Teesside project in England. Enron also purchased or constructed gas pipelines and power plants in South America.

Other new businesses, including international water development and broadband services, increased both Enron's market capitalization and its reputation as a world-class innovator. In 2000 Enron, confidently but also somewhat controversially, declared itself "the world's leading energy company." Enron's asset-light, Internet-based model, one Enron executive declared, was making

Samuel Insull

The rise and fall of Ken Lay echoes the career of Samuel Insull, the father of the modern electricity industry. In the early twentieth century Insull pioneered economies of scale by replacing isolated generating plants with large central station units that could electrify whole areas. Insull matched the consumption profile of the city and farm to run his units more efficiently and promote universal electricity service. He also used innovative financing techniques to meet the needs of his rapidly expanding businesses.

However, Insull's debt-heavy holding companies, controlling one-eighth of the national power market, proved unable to withstand the Great Depression and the machinations of his business rivals. Facing congressional critics and state and federal lawsuits, Insull pleaded innocent to criminal charges and put his whole career on trial. Insull was acquitted, and the faded industry icon lived out his years abroad in self-imposed exile.

Although the ultimate fate of Ken Lay in the wake of the Enron debacle is yet to be decided, the personal and business decisions of the two men offer historians a glimpse of how the past can illuminate the present. The two sagas, some 70 years apart, also serve as a warning of how quickly and profoundly fortunes can change in the market economy.

Samuel Insull arrives in court in 1934.

Enron employee Meredith Stewart sits with her belongings outside the Houston energy company's building on December 3, 2001, after the shattered and disgraced company laid off about 4,000 employees in the wake of its bankruptcy filing.

mid-October. The fabled EnronOnline was turned off, as customers could no longer bank on Enron credit. After an aborted merger attempt with a rival company, Enron filed for Chapter 11 bankruptcy. This, the largest such filing in U.S. history, was soon followed by mass layoffs. Enron began selling assets in 2002, leaving a collection of pipelines and power plants and an electric distribution company to satisfy creditor claims. The many lawsuits, congressional hearings, and Justice Department indictments involving Enron, its executives, its board of directors, and its accounting firm—Arthur Andersen—will keep Enron in the news for years.

Questionable accounting practices and risky capitalization schemes were only surface problems. Enron's series of bad investments that cost billions of dollars put the risky schemes into play in the first place. Indian authorities refused to honor their purchase agreements with Enron's large Dabhol power plant. A global water business, Azurix, was never profitable. Enron Broadband Services did not live up to its marketing hype. Other capital-intensive international investments were only marginally profitable.

The most surprising bust in Enron's portfolio concerned a core subsidiary, Enron Energy Services (EES). In a four-year period, EES entered into more than $30 billion of long-term contracts with large commercial and industrial users to manage their energy needs. The future profitability of the deals was estimated over the lives of the contracts, typically 10 years, and booked immediately as income under the rules of mark-to-market accounting. These profit estimates often proved to be self-serving and illusory, and Enron found itself with unprofitable contracts as actual costs were incurred and lower-than-expected revenues realized.

the integrated company model of the oil majors obsolete.

The Great Fall

Ken Lay's new vision, unveiled in early 2001, was to become "the world's leading company." A weakening stock price put the new vision on hold, and the unexpected resignation in August of Lay's hand-picked new chief executive officer, Jeffrey Skilling, pressured the stock price further. Lay's return as CEO sparked a temporary rally, but the end came quickly. A series of unfavorable financial disclosures led to a loss of investor confidence over a five-week period beginning in

Lessons

The public will remember Enron for mass layoffs, ruined retirement plans, unjust enrichment of top executives, aggressive or fraudulent accounting practices, conflicting congressional testimony, and court fights. Historians and business professors will

remember Enron for turning ambition into blind ambition and greed as Enron avoided and obscured its problems.

The failure to align executive and investor interests is an important aspect of the Enron debacle. Outside accountants did not accurately communicate the company's true financial position. Outside legal opinions were soft on Enron's controversial practices. Enron's management and board of directors did not communicate well and did not do what was necessary: set the proper incentives with appropriate checks and balances. Outside regulatory institutions were either not empowered to or failed to prevent malfeasance. Some of this failure may involve fraudulent activity, even in cases where no fraud is proven; whatever the facts, many business practices and regulatory rules will be scrutinized and quite possibly reformed in the wake of Enron's collapse.

Enron is also a textbook case of the perils of what is sometimes called political capitalism. Enron's major business lines were intimately connected with government regulation and government subsidies. The company was politically active with government at all levels. Enron's collapse has raised many questions about the influence of business on public policy.

Further Reading

Bradley, Robert. *Oil, Gas, and Government: The U.S. Experience.* Lanham, Md.: Rowman & Littlefield, 1996.

Hershey, Robert. "The Maverick Who Transformed an Industry." *New York Times,* 30 December 1984, F21.

McLean, Bethany. "Why Enron Went Bust." *Fortune,* 24 December 2001, 58–68.

Schumpeter, Joseph. *Capitalism, Socialism, and Democracy.* Boston: Unwin Paperbacks, 1987.

—*Robert L. Bradley Jr.*

Enron vice president Sherron Watkins (left) watches former Enron CEO Jeffrey Skilling (right) testify before a Senate Commerce subcommittee investigating the firm's collapse. Also shown is Skilling's attorney Bruce Hiler (center).

Entrepreneurship

Entrepreneurship is at the heart of the free enterprise system. At its heart, free enterprise combines different resources to provide goods and services to others. This includes traditional businesses that sell ordinary items, inventors developing new products, or not-for-profit agencies that, for example, provide disaster relief. Entrepreneurship is the engine that provides the new goods and services, job creation, and opportunity that make free enterprise so appealing.

The free market is based on two ideas. The first is that all people are free to trade as they please. Consumers and producers operate according to the laws of supply and demand and make their own decisions using their best judgment. The second premise is that of greed. Economists dating back to Adam Smith have shown that both consumers and producers make exchanges with the intention of making themselves better off.

Entrepreneurs are central to both of these ideas. Most operate in hopes of making a profit to enhance their well-being. However, because consumers are free to choose, producers must find ways to entice them to trade with them voluntarily. This combination of motives explains why entrepreneurs are the main source of innovation and creativity in an economy. Businesspeople must please their customers to be successful while making a profit. Achieving that result requires offering better products and services at lower prices.

Kinds of Entrepreneurship

Many of history's most famous entrepreneurs were inventors who created a new product. Thomas Edison is a prominent example. He became famous and wealthy by inventing dozens of new products, including the lightbulb and record player. Henry Ford took the example of Edison one step further. He did not invent the car, but he developed and refined a method to mass-produce cars through an assembly line. His Model A and Model T cars were built in large numbers, lowering their cost and leading to the adoption of the automobile for personal transportation.

Another path to success is finding methods to make existing products better or easier to use. Bill Gates became famous and wealthy through innovating in the computer industry. He and his partner, Paul Allen, collaborated to create software that offered a standard, reasonably easy-to-use operating system for personal computers.

Other entrepreneurs become successful by finding new ways to sell. Sam Walton, the founder of Wal-Mart, focused on improving management of department stores. His strategies included building large numbers of identical stores, computerizing inventory systems, and ordering goods in large quantities from manufacturers at discounted rates. These innovations worked so well that Wal-Mart became the largest consumer retail company in the world because it could offer very low prices.

Silicon Valley

Several factors contribute to Silicon Valley being a perfect incubator for entrepreneurs. First is its proximity to institutions of higher learning, including Stanford University and University of California at Berkeley, both leading schools in computer science, business, and engineering. Professors and students frequently start new businesses as the product of research or course work.

The most famous example of a company emerging from academia is Hewlett-Packard. Its founders were trained at Stanford and received valuable guidance in the development of the company and its products from a former professor. The company went from a garage start-up to the world's largest producer of personal computers and began the technological boom in Silicon Valley.

Universities also attract young, talented individuals with bold new ideas. This was a perfect match for the young computer industry. The field was wide open, with abundant opportunities for innovation that provided a natural outlet for entrepreneurial energy. Another advantage of the area was the relaxed culture. Internet start-up firms became famous for casual clothing, in-house chefs, and other luxuries unheard of in most businesses. This helped companies attract and retain talented programmers in an environment where ideas were critical to success.

Despite all of these advantages, even Silicon Valley is not immune to the ups and downs of business. After three decades of rapid expansion, the computer industry experienced a speculative bubble, or period of unsustainable growth, driven by an investor mania for anything related to the Internet. The bubble burst in 2000 after investors realized that many of the new companies had no ability to make profits. Hundreds of companies developing Internet applications or other technology quickly went out of business. In their enthusiasm, investors had overlooked a fundamental piece of business wisdom: invest only in companies that have a solid business plan.

Job and Wealth Creation

This process of innovation and creativity leads to another reason why entrepreneurs are important. The graph on page 426 shows that more than half of all workers in the United States work for a company that employs fewer than 100 workers. An additional 25 percent work for companies with fewer than 500 employees. Taken together, almost 80 percent of workers in the United States are employed by small or moderate-sized businesses, the vast majority of which are owned by entrepreneurs. Only about 20 percent of Americans work in medium or large businesses, which tend to be corporations.

The graph on page 427 details the percentage of new jobs created by each size of business. It is a common misperception that the majority of Americans work for large companies that do the majority of hiring (and firing). In fact, businesses with fewer than 500 workers created 88 percent of all new jobs in 1995.

Most Americans work for small businesses and these small businesses create the vast majority of new jobs. Larger companies play a different role in the economy. They became big companies by mass marketing, or selling products on a large scale, to generate sizable profit. Thus, they focus their energies on improving their current product or offering others with large profit potentials. Prescription drug companies are one example: they focus on products that many people

The National Foundation for Teaching Entrepreneurship gives awards for Young Entrepreneur of the Year. In 1999 the winners were Jasmine Angelica Jordan, 15, of Morris Heights, New York, and Daniel Miller, Jr., 11, of Pittsburgh, Pennsylvania. Jordan won for her magazine, Tools For Living, *and Miller won for his printing business,* Custom Postcards.

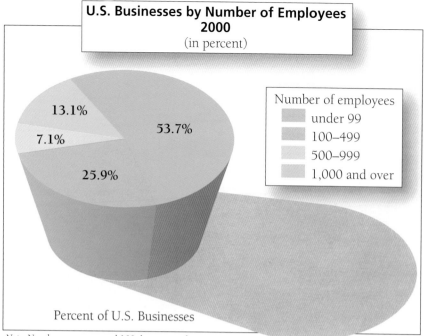

U.S. Businesses by Number of Employees 2000
(in percent)

13.1%

7.1%

53.7%

25.9%

Number of employees
- under 99
- 100–499
- 500–999
- 1,000 and over

Percent of U.S. Businesses

Note: Numbers may not total 100 due to rounding.
Source: Statistical Abstract of the United States.

The importance of small entrepreneurial firms is shown in the graph above—more than half of all U.S. workers are employed by small businesses.

can use but that are too expensive for smaller businesses to develop.

The strategies of large businesses explain the differences in the graph. Large firms create fewer jobs because they operate on a large scale with mature products. Rather than hire and fire many employees, large firms tend to shift production over time. Their numbers are also less dramatic because they can use mass production more efficiently and so may not need to hire as many workers.

Entrepreneurship offers a path to success for anyone willing to take the financial and personal risks. Anyone of any age, race, educational attainment, or gender can

start a business. This variety of ideas and approaches serves society as a whole.

Entrepreneurship is also the main method for achieving economic success in America. The majority of millionaires in the United States have not inherited their wealth: they are successful entrepreneurs who operate mundane businesses like dry cleaning, asphalt paving, and insect extermination. Wally Amos, an African American entrepreneur from New York, is a famous example. He started Famous Amos cookies in 1975 equipped with a recipe and a strong work ethic. Amos became financially successful and famous without a college degree or formal business training.

Is Small Better?

The benefits of starting one's own business are well known. Entrepreneurs are their own bosses, make all of the decisions, and can claim the credit for their success. Small companies also have two advantages over their larger competition. First, they can focus on small markets that bigger companies ignore for lack of profit potential. Overnight delivery services and plain paper copiers are both examples of products that entrepreneurs developed for niche markets.

Second, small companies can adapt to change quickly. As most are owned by one or two people, they can alter their hours of operation, product lines, prices, and other strategies very rapidly. Larger firms recognize flexibility's value and often structure parts of their businesses to so operate.

The challenges in entrepreneurship are daunting. The difficulties are reflected in one statistic: 90 percent of the businesses created each year go bankrupt. Poor management is one reason for the low success rate. Entrepreneurs must understand their business, communicate well with customers, understand marketing, and be competent at a number of other areas. Very few people are strong in all of these areas and, consequently, make bad decisions.

Another problem for entrepreneurs is the tremendous amount of time required to start and run a business. A new business

A lot of people come to me and say "I want to be an entrepreneur." And I go "Oh that's great, what's your idea?" And they say "I don't have one yet." And I say "I think you should go get a job as a busboy or something until you find something you're really passionate about because it's a lot of work." I'm convinced that about half of what separates the successful entrepreneurs from the nonsuccessful ones is pure perseverance. It is so hard. You put so much of your life into this thing. There are such rough moments in time that I think most people give up. I don't blame them. It's really tough and it consumes your life. . . . Unless you have a lot of passion about this, you're not going to survive. You're going to give it up. So you've got to have an idea, or a problem or a wrong that you want to right that you're passionate about, otherwise you're not going to have the perseverance to stick it through. I think that's half the battle right there.

—Steve Jobs, Smithsonian Oral History interview, 1995

an easily take 12 or more hours each day and often results in owners becoming burned out and quitting.

The leading cause of small business failure is inadequate funding. Banks and other lending institutions are very aware that most businesses are not successful and often refuse to extend loans. Thus, most entrepreneurs must use their own savings or borrow from friends and relatives. Both sources are often very limited and run out before the business develops.

Other sources of funding for new businesses include loans from state or local government. Successful new businesses create jobs, pay taxes, and provide other benefits; thus, governments have created many lending programs to encourage the development of small businesses.

Another source of funding is called venture capital. These are loans offered by businesses that specialize in investing in new companies. In return for providing funds and advice, the venture capital companies receive a portion of ownership. Venture capital is a fundamental element in the world's leading entrepreneurial region: Silicon Valley in northern California (see box on page 424). This region experienced two periods of explosive growth, in the 1980s with the advent of the personal computer and in the 1990s with the expansion of the Internet.

Starting a Business

When starting a new business, a solid business plan is imperative. This document outlines the product or service to be offered, how much it will cost to start and run the business, and so on. Business plans have two major uses: the plan requires the entrepreneur to create a strategy for success, which greatly improves prospects; the plan can be made available when applying for additional funding. If convincing, a well-conceived and thorough business plan can convince others of potential success.

Obtaining adequate funding and the process of planning can present a major barrier to creating a business. One common solution is to create a partnership. Partners

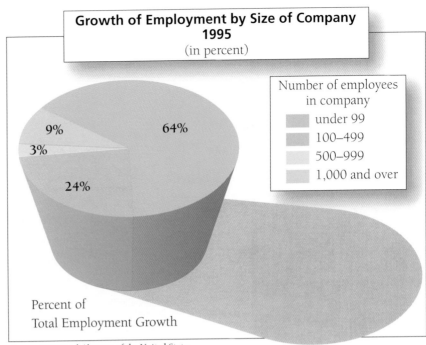

Growth of Employment by Size of Company 1995
(in percent)

Number of employees in company
- under 99
- 100–499
- 500–999
- 1,000 and over

9%
3%
64%
24%

Percent of Total Employment Growth

Source: Statistical Abstract of the United States.

may bring a variety of skills, additional funding, and a reduction in the workload to a business. The partnership business model is very common in the legal and medical professions. Partnerships come with drawbacks, however. Partners may disagree about business decisions. Many businesses fail or break up because of management discord. Other problems include limited funding and issues of legal liability.

Another solution is offered by franchises. Essentially franchises provide the opportunity to buy your own pre-made business. H&R Block, McDonald's, and Midas Mufflers are all franchises. Franchising offers advantages to both parties. The entrepreneurs purchase a business with name recognition, an established business plan, and already existing expertise in advertising. In return, the corporations receive payment for the name, a portion of all profits in the future, and the ability to easily expand. This is demonstrated by Subway Subs and McDonald's—each has more than 10,000 locations worldwide.

Entrepreneurship and Government

The opportunities for business and the business climate play a central role in the success and vitality of a country. The world's

Individual entrepreneurs can take credit for their enormous contribution to overall growth in employment in the United States.

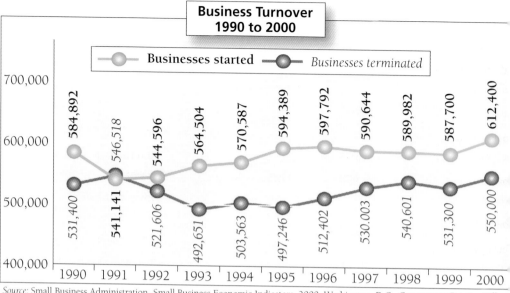

**Business Turnover
1990 to 2000**

- ○ Businesses started
- ● Businesses terminated

Year	Businesses started	Businesses terminated
1990	584,892	531,400
1991	546,518	541,141
1992	544,596	521,606
1993	564,504	492,651
1994	570,587	503,563
1995	594,389	497,246
1996	597,792	512,402
1997	590,644	530,003
1998	589,982	540,601
1999	587,700	531,300
2000	612,400	550,000

The failure rate for new businesses is high; each year nearly as many businesses end as are started.

Source: Small Business Administration, Small Business Economic Indicators, 2000, Washington, D.C., Government Printing Office 2000, http://www.sba.gov/advo/stats/sbei00.pdf (January 13, 2003).

wealthiest nations share a strong private sector featuring hard working, talented risk takers.

The United States and Hong Kong consistently lead the world in living standards. Both countries encourage entrepreneurship through relatively low taxes, limited government intervention, and strong protections for property rights. The last are especially important because they ensure that citizens can keep any wealth they accrue.

In general, economists have found that as property rights erode and taxes increase, the economic growth and living standards of nations decline. The most prominent example is North Korea, which drastically limits entrepreneurship and property rights. North Korea consistently experiences famine and other economic problems, in part because citizens lack incentives to become economically productive.

Entrepreneurship is an expression of optimism and self-confidence. While most businesses fail, those that succeed offer new goods and services and create the majority of new jobs each year. This process of competition and innovation is the central engine of economic progress.

Web Resources on Entrepreneurship

www.sba.gov is the home page of the federally run Small Business Administration, which offers a wide range of helpful materials.

www.startupbiz.com presents resources on creating a business plan, marketing, and other helpful items for starting your own business.

www.yeo.org is the home page of the Young Entrepreneurs Organization, a nonprofit educational organization for business owners under 40.

www.entreworld.org provides a variety of resources for entrepreneurs of all industries.

www.tannedfeet.com offers resources for entrepreneurs in the business, legal, and financial areas.

www.aeeg.org is the home page of the American Entrepreneurs for Economic Growth, a group focused on supporting government legislation that benefits the entrepreneurial communities and promotes economic growth.

www.yte.org, the Web site of the Youth Tech Entrepreneurs, encourages students to use their technical and academic skills to pursue entrepreneurial opportunities.

www.homeeducator.com provides resources for entrepreneurs in the home education and family services arenas.

Further Reading

Lewis, Michael. *The New New Thing: A Silicon Valley Story.* New York: Penguin Publishing, 2001.

Newman, Cathy. "Silicon Valley: Inside the Dream Incubator." *National Geographic Magazine,* December 2001. Also available: http://magma.nationalgeographic.com/ngm/0112/features.html (January 8, 2003).

Norman, Jan. *What No One Ever Tells You about Starting Your Own Business: Real Life Start-Up Advice from 101 Successful Entrepreneurs.* Chicago: Upstart Publishing, 1999.

Patsula, Peter J. *Successful Business Planning in 30 Days: A Step-by-Step Guide for Writing a Business Plan and Starting Your Own Business.* 2nd ed. New York: Patsula Media, 2002.

Paulson, Ed, and John Katzman. *The Complete Idiot's Guide to Starting Your Own Business.* 3rd ed. New York: Alpha Books, 2000.

—*David Long*

Glossary

absolute prices Prices measured in dollars, unadjusted for the effects of inflation.

asset Something of value. See encyclopedia entry, Assets and Liabilities.

balance sheet Document that summarizes the assets and liabilities of a business at a given time. See encyclopedia entry.

bankruptcy Legal process that allows a company or individual to restructure debts. See encyclopedia entry.

barriers to entry Factors discouraging competition in a market.

best practice Standard of comparison used in businesses that takes companies or individuals who operate most efficiently as a benchmark.

bondholders Individuals or entities that own bonds.

capital, human Skills and experience of workers.

capital, intellectual Knowledge used in production of a good or service.

capital, physical Tools used to produce and distribute goods and services.

capitalization The funding of business operations or growth.

Chapter 11 bankruptcy Legal proceeding that permits a business to continue to operate while restructuring finances and paying creditors. See encyclopedia entry, Bankruptcy.

commercial paper Short-term loan made to businesses.

cost-effectiveness Efficiency of using money in a particular way.

credit rating Assessment of likelihood of an individual, company, or government repaying its debts.

economies of scale Declining average cost of production that results from increasing output. See encyclopedia entry.

embezzlement Unlawfully taking company property (usually money) for personal use.

encryption Encoding information.

entrepreneurship Combining different resources to make goods or services available to others. See encyclopedia entry.

e-signature Electronic equivalent of a person's signature.

fiscal policy Attempting to manage economic expansions and contractions by adjusting government spending to stabilize incomes and economic performance. See encyclopedia entry.

flexible specialization Production method whereby individuals or teams use technology to produce large amounts of specialized goods.

grant Public or private donated funds used to support groups or individuals in specific efforts.

gross domestic product (GDP) Total output of goods and services in a country in one year. See encyclopedia entry.

identity theft Fraudulent use of the name and personal information of someone else; for example, to apply for credit cards.

inflation Period of rising prices. See encyclopedia entry.

infrastructure Transportation, communication, educational, and financial systems of a country. See encyclopedia entry.

Internet service provider (ISP) Company that provides Internet access to its customers.

investment Present use of resources to enable greater production in the future. See encyclopedia entry.

laissez-faire Policy of minimal government interference in an economy.

liability Any claim or debt against an individual or business. See encyclopedia entry.

market capitalization Total value of a corporation's outstanding shares.

mass production Use of machines to produce goods in large numbers.

monopoly Type of market that involves only one seller. See encyclopedia entry.

natural monopoly Situation in which competition does not result in cheaper goods or services; rather one firm is able to provide a good or service at lowest cost to consumers. See encyclopedia entry, Monopoly.

oligopoly Market dominated by a few sellers.

opportunity cost Alternatives that are forgone when a choice is made. See encyclopedia entry.

partnership Business structure with two or more individuals as owners. See encyclopedia entry.

privatization Sale of government providers of goods and services to private sector. See encyclopedia entry.

protocol Generally accepted method or standard.

proved reserves Supplies of a natural resource confirmed by geologic study.

purchasing power Amount of goods and services that can be purchased with a given amount of money.

racketeering Conducting a business using dishonest or criminal methods.

retained earnings Profits a business can use to fund further operations.

shareholders Owners of stock in a corporation.

stakeholders Active participants in corporate decisions.

tax credit Legislation that reduces tax liabilities for specified expenses; for example, expenses associated with pollution reduction may be partly offset by a tax credit.

venture capital Private funds used to start or expand a business. See encyclopedia entry.

Index

Page numbers in **boldface** type indicate article titles. Page numbers in *italic* type indicate illustrations or other graphics.